Who Can You Trust With Your Money?

Who Can You Trust
With Your Money?

GET THE HELP YOU NEED NOW
AND AVOID DISHONEST ADVISORS

BONNIE KIRCHNER, CFP®, MST

Vice President, Publisher: Tim Moore
Associate Publisher and Director of Marketing: Amy Neidlinger
Executive Editor: Jim Boyd
Editorial Assistant: Myesha Graham
Development Editor: Russ Hall
Operations Manager: Gina Kanouse
Senior Marketing Manager: Julie Phifer
Publicity Manager: Laura Czaja
Assistant Marketing Manager: Megan Colvin
Cover Designer: Alan Clements
Managing Editor: Kristy Hart
Project Editor: Anne Goebel
Copy Editor: Language Logistics, LLC
Proofreader: Leslie Joseph
Indexer: Lisa Stumpf
Senior Compositor: Jake McFarland
Manufacturing Buyer: Dan Uhrig

© 2010 by Pearson Education, Inc.

Publishing as FT Press
Upper Saddle River, New Jersey 07458

FT Press offers excellent discounts on this book when ordered in quantity for bulk purchases or special sales. For more information, please contact U.S. Corporate and Government Sales, 1-800-382-3419, corpsales@pearsontechgroup.com. For sales outside the U.S., please contact International Sales at international@pearson.com.

Company and product names mentioned herein are the trademarks or registered trademarks of their respective owners.

Printed in the United States of America

First Printing February 2010

ISBN-10: 0-13-703365-6
ISBN-13: 978-0-13-703365-2

Pearson Education LTD.
Pearson Education Australia PTY, Limited.
Pearson Education Singapore, Pte. Ltd.
Pearson Education North Asia, Ltd.
Pearson Education Canada, Ltd.
Pearson Educatión de Mexico, S.A. de C.V.
Pearson Education—Japan
Pearson Education Malaysia, Pte. Ltd.

Library of Congress Cataloging-in-Publication Data
Kirchner, Bonnie, 1967-
   Who can you trust with your money? : get the help you need now and avoid dishonest advisors / Bonnie Kirchner.
      p. cm.
   Includes index.
   ISBN 978-0-13-703365-2 (hardback : alk. paper) 1. Financial planners—United States. 2. Investment advisors—United States. I. Title.
   HG179.5.K57 0010
   332.6—dc22
                                    2009042822

*Who Can You Trust With Your Money is dedicated first and
foremost to my parents, Ted and Kathy Kirchner, who gave
me the tools at a very young age to become a financially
responsible adult so that I could in turn help others. Without
their love and support and that of my sister, Peggy Cavanaugh,
and my brother, Eric Kirchner, my niece and nephew, Katie
and Sean Cavanaugh, as well as my truly amazing friends,
colleagues, and clients, I don't know how I could have found
my footing after my ex-husband's dramatic confession, along
with all that ensued, and emerge on the other side stronger,
more compassionate, open and loving, and better equipped to
deliver financial education with passion. I am forever grateful
to all of you. My mother-in-law, Mary Frances Bleidt, who
has always inspired me with her dedication, passion, creativity,
and inner strength, continues to do so despite being a
victim herself. I thank her and her family, including my
step-children, for being so supportive of me despite all of
the turmoil introduced into their own lives.*

Contents

Foreword xi

Acknowledgments xiii

About the Author xv

Introduction xvii

Chapter 1   Recent Investment Scams 1

Bradford C. Bleidt 1

Bernard Madoff 8

Chapter 2   What Is Financial Planning? 15

Chapter 3   The Meaning Behind Advisor Designations
and Licenses 21

Chapter 4   Advisor Compensation 31

Chapter 5   Deciphering Fee Structures 35

Portfolio Development and Asset
Management 35

Financial Planning 36

Stocks, Bonds, and Exchange Traded Funds . . . 36

Mutual Funds 37

Variable Annuities 39

Indexed Annuities 41

Insurance 41

Chapter 6   Finding Additional Fees 43

Managed and/or Brokerage 43

Variable Annuities 44

Mutual Funds 45

Exchange Traded Funds and Index Funds . . . 46

Chapter 7 Financial Products and Advisor
Compensation 47

Investment-Related 48

Insurance Coverage 49

Financial Planning 50

Chapter 8 Statements, Communications, and the
"Dreaded" Prospectus 51

Statements 51

Prospectuses—Mutual and Exchange
Traded Funds 53

Shareholder Updates and Annual Reports . . . 55

Prospectuses—Variable Annuities 56

Standard Charges (on Most Contracts) 56

Rider Electives 57

Proxy Materials 57

Chapter 9 The Roles of Various Financial
Institutions 59

Investments in Insurance Products 61

Investment Management and Investment
Product Sales 63

The Broker/Dealer 63

The Custodian 64

CONTENTS

The Federal Deposit Insurance
Company 65

The Securities Investment Protection
Corporation (SIPC) 66

Chapter 10 Understanding What You Need 67

Chapter 11 Choosing Advisors to Consider 77

Chapter 12 Choosing Candidates to Interview 81

Chapter 13 Interviewing Candidates 85

Preparing for the Meeting 85

During the Meeting 92

After the Meeting 97

Chapter 14 Spotting Red Flags: Advisors to Avoid 101

The Name and Information
Gathering Phase 101

During the Meeting 104

After the Meeting 106

Advisors to Avoid 107

Chapter 15 The Rules of Engagement 111

Chapter 16 Maintenance of the Advisor–Client
Relationship 127

Chapter 17 Activity 131

Chapter 18 Accessibility 135

Chapter 19 The Dysfunctional Relationship 137

Chapter 20 Criminal Versus Non-Criminal
Behavior 143

Chapter 21 Filing a Complaint 149

Appendix A Consumer Resources 155

Credit Ratings Agencies 163

Appendix B Glossary 167

Index 187

Foreword

by Steven J. J. Weisman

If you think that you are too smart to ever be the victim of an investment scam, then this book is not for you. And I wish you luck, because that is what you are going to need in the precarious financial times we are living in. Scam artists are the only criminals we refer to as artists, and they have earned that title. No matter how knowledgeable you are, no matter how financially sophisticated you may think you are, you are a potential victim. As we learned from the Bernie Madoff scandal, intelligent and savvy people can easily fall prey to these financial predators. The only defense is education.

Bonnie Kirchner provides that education in this book that is so critically important in today's economy. Bonnie is a CERTIFIED FINANCIAL PLANNER™ professional. She also has a Bachelor of Science degree in Financial Counseling and Planning from Purdue University and a Master in Taxation degree from Bentley University. But a lot of people have credentials—Bonnie is also a communicator. She can take complex financial information and make it understandable. She was a fixture on the Boston radio and television scene providing financial information to millions of people for ten years.

She also knows what it feels like to be a victim of a scam artist, because before there was Bernie Madoff, there was Brad Bleidt: a charming, clever, financial planner and advisor who ran one of the country's largest Ponzi investment scams for years until his house of cards—like Bernie Madoff's—fell. Brad Bleidt was so charming that Bonnie Kirchner married him. And until the fateful day that his Ponzi scheme unraveled, Bonnie had no idea what he was doing. Brad Bleidt was tried and convicted and is presently serving time in federal prison. His many victims, too, are in prison, except theirs is the financial prison that resulted from many of them losing their life savings to this criminal who appeared so trustworthy.

How do Bernie Madoff and Brad Bleidt happen? How is our financial system able to be exploited by predators like them? And perhaps more importantly, what do you need to know to keep yourself from becoming the victim of the next Bernie Madoff?

In this book, Bonnie provides you with the critical knowledge you need to protect yourself from financial scam artists. She tells you what to look for. In this book, she gives you good, practical advice that you can use to make yourself a better educated investor. She knows that when it comes to looking for a helping hand in matters of finance, the best place to look is at the end of your own arm. As we learned in the Madoff affair, you can't depend on the government to protect you from such villains.

But there is plenty of financial risk that we all face, even when we are not dealing with scam artists. If you are going to play the game, you have to know the rules. Bonnie clearly explains the confusing array of financial advisor designations. She also lets you know just how financial products work. And she lets you in on how financial advisors are compensated. Is your financial advisor working for you or for himself or herself with inappropriate fees hidden in fine print? Rarely, if ever, is there anything "fine" in fine print. Bonnie cuts through the fine print and lets you know how to work with the good, honest, financial advisors as a knowledgeable, informed consumer. This book will empower you.

Steven J. J. Weisman is an attorney and provides weekly legal commentaries on the nationally syndicated "Doug Stephan's Good Day" show. Steve is also host of the syndicated radio show "A Touch of Grey" heard throughout the country. Presently, he is a Senior Lecturer at Bentley University and is the legal editor and a columnist for Talkers Magazine. *His most recent books include* The Truth About Buying Annuities *and* The Truth About Protecting Your IRAs and 401(k)s.

Acknowledgments

Thank you to authors Steven J. J. Weisman and Nancy Hunter Denney who gave me the inspiration and courage to take the big step getting started on this project and provided so much guidance, support, and laughter through the entire process. I am very grateful for not only the informational content contributions provided by Charlie Clapp and Susan Gordon, but also their important friendships. I am, without end, grateful to executive editor, Jim Boyd, and Pearson Education, Inc. for believing in me and this project; as well as my colleagues Julie Gebert and David Whelan, for seeing me through the homestretch.

To my dearest girlfriends, Meg, Katie, Michelle, and Amy who supported me in ways I couldn't even fathom, so many times and so unexpectedly, I owe you a world of gratitude for your unconditional friendship. Thank you to Pat, Katie, Patrick, Matthew, and Anna for being my family away from my family; Johnny M for putting a roof over my head and my stuff, what was left of it anyway; and the bright and talented women of WKRP, as well as the entire J24 community who remind me on a regular basis how lucky I really am. To Laurie, Dennis, Ken, NV, and so many others: I couldn't have gotten here without you.

My former colleagues at WBIX and FPPS, I miss your inspiring wisdom, knowledge, and creativity every day but am grateful to have had the experience of working with you all. You amaze me in the ways so many of you reached out to me even though you had lost your own jobs and worse. That I will never forget, especially Nancy and John for taking such good care of my dear Rudy and his ailments over these past years and of course, Jimmie, for always being my confidant, mentor, and friend ever since I met my now ex-husband. I also thank Alan Rose Sr. and Alan Rose Jr. as well as Karen Schwartzman for guiding me through the most difficult period of my life. Your efforts to keep me out of harm's way are most appreciated.

To my inspiring grandmothers, great aunt, and best friend, Patrick, my thoughts are with you every day.

About the Author

Bonnie Kirchner is a CERTIFIED FINANCIAL PLANNER™ professional with a Master of Science degree in taxation from Bentley University in Waltham, Massachusetts. Ms. Kirchner received her Bachelor of Science degree in financial counseling and planning from Purdue University in West Lafayette, Indiana, and has been practicing since 1990. Early in her career, Bonnie became passionate about educating individuals on financial topics. A frequent speaker about retirement, estate, long-term care, investing, and education planning concepts in the Boston area, she also contributed financial content to various publications and radio programming. Ms. Kirchner eventually began hosting the financial talk show "Handling Change" and most recently co-anchored "Early Exchange," a morning-drive business magazine heard on Boston's business radio station. Ms. Kirchner also served as the financial reporter for Boston's CBS affiliate, delivering financial information each weekday morning live from the Boston Stock Exchange. Bonnie is the founder and owner of Even Keel Financial Services, LLC and $ea Change Financial Education, LLC, and is an Investment Advisor Representative of Cambridge Investment Research Advisors, Inc., an SEC Registered Investment Advisor. Bonnie Kirchner, Even Keel Financial Services, and $ea Change Financial Education are not affiliated with Cambridge Investment Research, Inc. Bonnie lives and maintains her practice in Marion, Massachusetts.

Introduction

I find most people learn best from mistakes made. And if you can learn from those of others, well, all the better. Working as a financial advisor and broadcaster for nearly 20 years, I have seen the good, the bad, and the ugly of mistake making, and I've made many of my own along the way. In fact, some of my own misjudgments have resulted in fundamental modifications of the advice I give others. Fortunately, most people will not find themselves in the same situation I did, but most of us will experience financial shifts and changes throughout our lifetimes. Organizing your finances in a way that will enable you to easily react to and handle change will put you in a much better position to take on any accompanying emotional turmoil. Gaining and maintaining control and flexibility over your finances, rather than allowing them to control you, gives you the power of solid decision making, especially in times of crisis. Without this element of control, changes are handled in a reactionary manner, and inevitably mistakes, frequently expensive ones, are made.

It was the dramatic direction change in my life that inspired me to try to help protect others by arming them with education. For years I had been reporting on the corporate and mutual fund scandals, disgusted at how many people were being hurt and how much money was being wasted. I would cringe every time I had to do another story on a corrupt financial planner taking advantage of unsuspecting citizens, discrediting the field to which I had dedicated so much of my life. Little did I know, my own career and life were encased in a bubble of deception that was getting ready to burst in a very big way.

On November 10, 2004, I was on top of the world. My husband and I were commemorating a major milestone for the radio station we worked so hard to build. Finally we were taking programming twenty-four hours, seven days a week. I couldn't have been more satisfied with my career, despite the grueling hours and the toll it was taking on my personal life. The morning after the celebration our company's receptionist came to my office door with a package. It had my husband's handwriting on it, and I think we both drew the conclusion that it was an attempt by Brad to be romantic. "Too little, too late" was what I was thinking. Our marriage had been deteriorating since its inception five years prior, and I had finally asked for a divorce in September.

I opened the package and found a small recording device with a sticker pointing to the Play button, which said "press here" on it, once again, in Brad's handwriting. I hit play.

"Hello, Bonnie, it's me. Straight to the chase here. Tragic, tragic news," I heard Brad say. My immediate thought was that something terrible had happened to one of my step-children. I could never have imagined the tale that was about to unfold out of that tiny recording device.

"I am guilty of some very hideous crimes. I've been stealing clients' monies for roughly 20 years. And we're talking about tens and tens of millions of dollars; I mean we're talking about very, very big monies. And today a wire for the Greek Church is supposed to hit for 1.5 million, which does not exist because I've stolen it. So everything is going to hit the fan today. Obviously, the monthly statements that I was generating are fraudulent. The monies don't exist in those statements. It's a great big Ponzi scheme because I've also been doing direct deposits to quite a few clients on a monthly basis using ACH [Automated Clearing House]. What I would end up doing is just signing up new clients, having the checks made payable to APAM [Allocation Plus Asset Management Corp—Brad Bleidt's investment management firm], and deposited them in a Sovereign bank account. I don't understand how I could have gotten myself into this thing. It was just one little step at a time that got bigger and bigger and bigger and then the stakes got higher and higher and higher, and it just got totally out of control. I did notify the SEC and told them that nobody had any clue what I was doing, and I was totally responsible for everything and there's no way that anybody could have known what I was doing."

I truly could not even fathom what Brad was saying. I could not imagine him stealing from people, nor could I believe he would attempt to take his own life as he indicated in his confessional tape to me. It would take me days to realize that what I heard was actually true. The Brad I knew was not capable of hurting anyone. He loved people, was extremely social with and attentive to his clients and employees, and was passionate about the business he was building. It didn't make any sense to me whatsoever. I thought he had gone off the deep end and that he was delusional. But I was not the only one to receive a message from Brad that day. Tapes were sent to key employees, family members, and the Securities and Exchange Commission.

It took a few days, but reality eventually started to sink in when I began seeing Brad's photo on the front page of the papers and on the news. I still couldn't believe he would steal, especially from people of whom he was so seemingly fond. My thoughts drifted to his clients, from one to another, especially those I knew personally, wondering how Brad could financially ruin these people who loved him and depended upon him to steer them to and through their retirements. But he had confessed to his own mother from his hospital bed that she, too, was a victim. Then my mind turned to my own clients; those for whom I was responsible for guiding and helping achieve their own financial goals. I knew their money was with our custodian, because I looked at the statements every month and could access all of their accounts via the online system. I knew there was no way he could have accessed their accounts. But did they know? Were they waking up on Sunday morning to see my husband's face on the front pages of their papers or turning on the news, hearts sinking at the thought that they, too, were victims? I knew I had to reach them as soon as possible. I also wanted to be as supportive as possible to Brad's mother, who was not only dealing with the attempted suicide of her son, but also the fact that he had stolen her money, too. Even with this latest blow, she was exhibiting incredible strength and being amazingly supportive of me, but I knew she must be hurting in ways I would never know.

It is said that "you learn who your friends are" during periods like these, and I certainly did. I saw the very ugly side of others, including that of my ex-husband, a side that was beginning to be exposed that no one had ever even fathomed existed. It took over a year for Brad to stand trial. During that time I could've become homeless if it had not been for the generosity of my family and friends. I was relieved of many of our possessions. It is incredibly humbling to stand in a warehouse and watch strangers pick through items that were once part of your every day life, evaluating what things are worth and on what they might bid and, on top of it all, having it very publically broadcast through the media. I was also relieved of much of my savings, given that I was following my own advice and saving regularly in a joint brokerage account for my husband and me, trying to diversify our marital assets, assuming most of his money was being invested in his companies. I had put his name on my investment account; thus, the government appointed receiver felt strongly and possibly correctly, that half belonged to Brad. Though the proof existed that I alone contributed to the account, I was encouraged to settle and was told that the receiver's report was coming out and if I didn't cooperate, it would be stated that I was in possession of items believed to be purchased with stolen funds and that I was being uncooperative. I was also told the media would be interested in this public report. I assume the receiver's representative was aware that I very much wanted to get back to work on TV and radio and that I could not afford to have any bad publicity. As hard as it was, I had to think about my future. The only way I could move forward was by letting go of the past. Though I would never wish what I went through on anyone, it was life-changing in many positive ways. For the first time in my life I had to open up and accept the fact that I needed help. Prior to all of this, I was always "fine." I didn't need anyone's assistance and was somewhat of a loner. When my life exploded I was forced to acknowledge that the resulting mayhem was more than I could handle and allow my friends and family to help me in big and little ways.

The question that remains unanswered is: how could I have not known? After all, I was a financial advisor and a financial reporter; shouldn't I have somehow figured it all out? I have seen the questions on web blogs, and former colleagues have shared with me that they have been asked the same. As far as I know, Brad kept his demons locked up in special filing cabinets in his office, undiscovered by anyone including auditors from the National Association of Securities Dealers (now the Financial Industry Regulatory Authority) and the Securities and Exchange Commission. Our former president, CFO, Brad's executive assistant, and I came to the conclusion that it would have taken the perfect storm of conversation between the four of us to create suspicion for any of us about what Brad was actually doing. Do I wish I had picked up on clues that may have existed? Absolutely. As I said in my press statement, "I can't tell you how much I wish I had some idea of what was going on so that I might have acted to prevent it." I have no doubt in my mind that I would have turned him in if he wouldn't have done it himself, had I somehow learned the truth. I have dedicated my adult life to my profession and the people we serve and who trust us to look after their financial interests. Brad violated all of that. He is not the person I thought he was and with whom I fell in love and married. He was an imposter and a phony. The person I thought I knew so well certainly felt about the profession and clients the way I did. I never would have imagined he was capable of what he did; thus, it was impossible to notice clues that may have existed.

Though we worked together, our daily paths had few intersections. I had my clients, and he had his. Our staffs worked independently of each other as well. Ours were individual practices within the same business shell. Our offices were in separate buildings, and we kept very different hours. Our finances were kept separately too, with the exception of the joint brokerage account on which I had put his name. I always thought we were "the shoemaker's children," not tending to our own financial planning despite being in the business. However, ours was a second marriage for him, and he had children and I didn't; thus, financial planning was never a priority. With no prenuptial agreement, he had more to lose than I did, or so I thought. On the one occasion when finances were discussed, in regard to resources, he grew quite testy with me, so I didn't pursue it. I had expressed concerns about corporate expenses. He was indignant and strongly assured me things were covered by proceeds left to him by an insurance policy on his father's life, which he had invested and with which he had done quite well in the late nineties. I really didn't want money to be a source of conflict in our marriage, and I didn't want him to ever think I was in any way interested in what clearly belonged to him, so I accepted his heated and concise explanation. I was financially independent from him, and we were already having other issues that were much bigger as far as I was concerned, so it just wasn't worth it to me to press it. Perhaps I should have probed more, but our marriage was falling apart over more important things than money, so I left it alone. The truth is that there was never a reason presented to me, nor anyone else for that matter, to suspect that Brad was stealing from his clients.

I have always felt strongly about education, especially financial. Perhaps that is why I ended up in media. My position with Boston's CBS affiliate allowed me to reach a large audience in hopes that each morning I could pass on at least one small tidbit of information that might be helpful to someone. Each week I would write an educational article and field questions for the CBS4 website, even though I was not obligated to do so under my contract. I just wanted, and still do, to help empower people to take control over their financial futures. Am I in any way blaming the people who entrusted Brad with their life's savings? Absolutely not. After all, I too, was taken in by this con man.

The financial world is complicated. Even regulatory steps taken to help protect people add to the complexity for the average investor making them vulnerable to people like my ex-husband. The way Brad Bleidt took advantage of the people who trusted him is deplorable, but is it preventable? Despite the efforts of regulatory and enforcement entities, fraud is on the rise. Financial consumers need to educate themselves. Trying to put this book together made me realize how complicated the industry I entered into is and made me think, "How could the average investor know or understand all that I take for granted from 25 years of experience and education? It's no wonder people are so vulnerable to those looking to line their own pockets!" This is the start of my own effort to educate consumers on financial matters so that they may build their financial futures, starting with a solid foundation. Many people will need various advisors along the way. Choosing the right advisors and understanding how to work with them is critical to your own financial success.

QUICK TIPS

- A reluctance to discuss finances by one or both members of an interdependent couple can be a red flag of existing problems which, if not addressed, can snowball out of control. Concerns could range from overspending, gambling, and extreme frugality to, in the extreme case, participation in illegal activities.

- Open communication about finances with one's significant other is paramount to a healthy relationship and should not be ignored.

- A solid understanding of resources and obligations along with proper goal setting and planning can have tremendous "teambuilding" effects, promote financial efficiency, and prevent unpleasant surprises down the road.

- Proper financial planning for couples and families not only enhances each member's ability to spot potential problems but empowers them to handle issues, big or small, should they arise.

Chapter 1

Recent Investment Scams

~ Bradford C. Bleidt

You might imagine the typical scam artist to be slick and persuasive and possibly utilize high pressure sales tactics. This is not the case in many situations, which is why so often people get caught off guard. Most of us like to believe we are somewhat savvy and can spot a phony or sense if something is not quite right. It is because successful scam artists are so incredibly good at making people feel comfortable that they are able to execute without suspicion. This was certainly the case with my ex-husband, Bradford Chester Bleidt. Most of Brad's clients were people who viewed him as a son, brother, best friend, and/or confidant. His demeanor was a bit bumbling, which added to his charm. He was somewhat goofy and geeky, yet he could discuss his investment approach and what was happening in the markets in complex detail, inspiring confidence among his "investors." Those victimized genuinely liked Brad and enjoyed being around him, and Brad would do anything for his "clients." Until my world was torn apart, I never quite understood the frequent and lengthy personal conversations he had with clients, the unlimited access he granted to certain customers, and why dinners and events with others were so important. But I experienced first-hand the cult-like leader effect Brad had, especially among the local Masonic groups. Despite my early morning broadcasting hours, I was asked to attend events held by the Masons, which I did happily. They're a wonderful group of people and welcomed me. It was evident how the members felt about Brad and that

1

trust was not an issue. Of course, there was no question in my mind about the validity of the services Brad was performing for these people. The Brad Bleidt I knew was a talented, smart, innovative, and creative financial advisor. As far as I knew, these people were fortunate to be getting his time, something I received very little of as his wife. But as far as I knew we were working toward a greater goal, and in the later years I had fallen out of love with him, so I wasn't resentful of the time Brad spent supposedly helping people and building his independent financial planning and asset management firms.

Brad Bleidt had high standards for the financial advisors working at his firm, Financial Perspectives. He expected prospective planners to have the proper licenses and be working toward a professional designation, such as the CERTIFIED FINANCIAL PLANNER™ professional designee or Chartered Financial Analyst. Compliance seemed to be a huge priority at the firm, which paid off, given examinations performed by the NASD (now FINRA) and the SEC that resulted in no significant deficiencies. There were no black marks that a prospective client might discover and choose to go elsewhere or would potentially attract suspicion by regulatory agencies to dig a little deeper. As Brad admitted in a confessional tape sent to the SEC, "The big cover was that we ran a clean operation here other than me...just by being able to have a legitimate operation stand in front of my crimes so my, you know, my embezzlements, I was able to shield from purview anything that I did. Pretty...you know it is something to consider when client lists were requested during an audit; you know obviously the clients that I have embezzled from are never on the client list."

Each planner had his or her own clients. We were responsible for building our own businesses, albeit many of the opportunities to do so came through Financial Perspectives. Brad had been generous in helping get people, me included, started, though there were certain projects he kept to himself. It seemed obvious that Brad should be the planner assigned to work with the Masons as he was the only Masonic member of our organization.

Though Brad surrounded himself with intelligent people, he was clever in maintaining his team. Even his immediate planning staff members, those who might deal with client servicing and planning needs, had little experience with the intricacies of the financial services industry. It is my understanding they would never need to look up one of Brad's victim's client accounts, given that he took care of those clients himself. In one case, he became angry and irritated with his assistant because she had tried to actually help a client with an account issue. In another situation he moved an extremely talented and dedicated staff member off of his team and assigned her to assist the asset management staff in helping the other planners in our firm with their clients. Why? Because she had a financial services background. She was hired away from one of our former brokerage relationships, and she is extremely bright. I'm guessing he was concerned she would figure it all out.

Many people viewed Brad as a visionary in the financial services field. As with Bernard Madoff, I would not be surprised if many of Brad Bleidt's clients felt grateful to him for working with them and certainly for much of the extra interaction and attention he provided. He seemed to genuinely care for his clients like they were family. Perhaps part of him did feel that way given the concern he seemed to express in his suicide confessional tapes, or perhaps this was just a distraction technique. It is hard to say, but the betrayal his clients, family, friends, employees, and business associates experienced is a big part of the devastation beyond the financial consequences. His victims not only had to deal with the shock of being wiped out financially, but also the psychological effects of the betrayal by someone they considered a son, brother, friend, and/or confidant.

I am in no way suggesting that Brad's clients were ignorant and should have figured out what he was up to. I had the pleasure of meeting many of the people who were affected before his dramatic confession: I socialized with some and was good friends with others, not to mention his own family with whom I remain close. His victims include college professors, talented artists, attorneys, and extremely intelligent business people. His mother, who is also a victim of her son, is one of the brightest and most innovative people I've ever met. What these people had in common, as many investors with advisors do, is a lack of knowledge about how the investment industry works.

So how did he do it, and what can we learn from it? Though I don't know all of the details, I do have a better understanding why my husband felt the need to spend the first weekend of every month in the office. Because we were not getting along terribly well, I was grateful for his absence. His explanation was that there were certain clients of his who had become accustomed to monthly rather than quarterly performance statements and that it gave him a better perspective preparing these documents on a monthly basis. What I didn't know was that these were the *only* statements his clients were getting. Unlike my clients and those of every other planner in our firm who received monthly statements from the custodian we were using, Brad's clients only received the statements prepared by him and nothing from any established custodian. As he admitted to me after he was behind bars, Brad was modeling his "portfolios" with a full understanding of what had happened in the markets over the prior month. In this fashion, he was able to satisfy his clients with supposed reasonable returns, even during difficult times. Why would his clients question what he was doing? He seemed to be making money for them even when the market was not performing well. Perhaps this should be the first clue: when market conditions are not favorable and your portfolio is bucking the trend, perhaps it's not time to cheer but rather time to dig a little deeper and understand why. On top of that, if you are not receiving statements prepared but the institution that has possession of your assets, start digging until you understand why.

No confirmation? Though it is my understanding that Brad provided his clients with manufactured statements, as far as I know, he did not go as far as creating trading confirmations. What is a confirmation? If a financial representative executes a trade in your account by buying or selling something like a mutual fund, stock, or bond, a receipt of the transaction is generated and sent to the address of record. The confirmation is a valuable information piece that depicts how many shares were bought or sold and for how much. It also shows if any commissions or fees were charged. If Brad's clients were seeing transactions on their statements, had the accounts been legitimate, they would have also received these confirmations for the "trades" he was executing. So if you are looking at a statement that shows transactions, yet you never received a separate record of the trades being executed, start making some inquiries.

Another clue that existed for Brad's clients is the fact that, according to his confessional tapes, he had customers make checks payable to "Allocation Plus Asset Management Corp" rather than our custodian. As brokers, we are not typically allowed to accept client checks made payable to ourselves or our firms. The checks are usually made payable to the custodial firm that provides the SIPC insurance (Securities Investor Protection Corporation). The average consumer is unaware of this fact. Occasionally I would receive checks made payable to our planning firm, Financial Perspectives. After all, it seemed only natural for the client to make their investment check payable in this manner. Standard procedure in the event a client made a check payable to the wrong entity would be to immediately return it to the client. Yes, it is an inconvenience to the client, but it is a process of checks and balances to prevent people from running off with client money. In one instance I heard about a client of Brad's who made a check payable to the proper custodian. When he received the canceled check back from his bank, Brad had crossed out the name of the custodian and written in "APAM." If true, this should not only have been a red flag for the client but a major signal to the bank that something was not right. It is important to understand where your assets are going, whether or not they are insured, and what preventative measures are in place to protect you from the wrong person getting his hands on them.

It is my understanding that Brad, as he admitted to me after he was in jail, was able to access client assets when we changed broker/dealers. As registered reps, we must have a "home office" or a broker/dealer to handle trades and oversee the compliance for our business. They are often referred to as the home office because many of these entities have grown to provide many services for brokers, such as administrative training, marketing support, and so on. And why wouldn't they? The more the broker makes, the more the broker/dealer receives in compensation as the broker is typically paid out at a certain percentage of commissions and fees earned by the broker. The nature of the broker/dealer relationship is one of service, and brokers may change these relationships for a number of reasons. Our firm had a long-standing relationship with a particular broker/dealer based in the Boston area. Brad's discontent with this relationship had been growing over a number of years; all the while we were being wooed by other firms. When two of our top producers left Financial Perspectives, supposedly encouraged by the broker/dealer with which we were associated, Brad had had enough of the competitive relationship he had with our home office and triggered a move to a competitor. Despite everything being in place for execution, Brad was extremely nervous about the move. So much so, he backed out of my family's important trip to cheer on my sister in her first Hawaii Iron Man competition even though I had bought him a nonrefundable ticket. He claimed he was also nervous about flying after September

11th. The devastating attacks had happened a couple of weeks earlier. In a conversation after he was behind bars, he confessed he was able to gain access to some assets through our movements from broker/dealer to broker/dealer. This might explain why we changed our broker/dealer relationships twice within as many years. I don't know how as I didn't ask. As he explained to the SEC, he cashed out one client's account during one of these transitions and sent the funds to the client's bank account and then asked the client to write checks to APAM. So if your advisor is changing "broker/dealers" or "back offices" or "home offices," make it a point to understand why and be sure to ask about the custodian. Know what custodian you are leaving and where your assets are going, what insurance coverage and fees are involved, and ask for a sample statement if the custodian is also going to be changed. A move by your registered representative can be a good thing, but a little verification can go a long way toward sleeping at night knowing your funds are safe.

Finally, what about the 1099s? The custodian is also responsible for issuing you your tax documents, whether you have an individual, retirement, trust, education, or some other type of account. If you take money out of your IRA, you should get a 1099R from the custodian. Dividends, interest, and sales will be reported on the 1099. If you don't get one, there's a problem. If the IRS disagrees with the accuracy of your tax return in regard to investment or retirement accounts, there might be an issue that is worth investigating.

Though I have never discussed it with him, my suspicion with Brad is that it started small. In his confession to me, he claimed the fraud had been going on for 20 years, or 10 years before I met him, which means it started in the early to mid eighties. He would've been fairly new to Boston and trying to build a business and support a growing family. Though he was seemingly successful when I met him, he was always ambitious and wanted things to happen much quicker than they typically did. He had a tendency to talk about the future as if it were in the present. As he once explained to me; talking about the future in the present tense is how he would make things happen. Building a customer base does take time, and it's tough. This I know because I've done it. I imagine with the growing needs of his family combined with an unsteady income, Brad succumbed to using customer assets, probably those of his own family and with the full intention of returning them. I wouldn't be surprised if in the beginning he did return them. But the slippery slope was in place. Once executed successfully, it is likely the "borrowing" of client monies habitually became a way for Brad to fund his dreams more quickly than if he had been doing it legitimately. Again this is all speculation on my part. Brad, along with being narcissistic and having entitlement issues, also has an addictive personality as was demonstrated by his alcohol abuse and cigarette smoking. Knowing what I've learned since his confession, I wouldn't be surprised if the slippery slope turned into a giant snowball partly fueled by his own addictive tendencies. He is now serving an 11-year sentence in federal prison for his crimes. Many of his victims are serving a "life sentence," given that only pennies on the dollars lost were returned to them.

Bernard Madoff

As I speculated in regard to my ex-husband and the "snowball" effect in relation to his crimes, it may be that Bernard Madoff fell down the slippery slope in a similar but much larger fashion. In a June 2009 article in *Vanity Fair*, he is reported as saying to his secretary, Eleanor Squillari, "Well, you know what happens is, it starts out with you taking a little bit, maybe a few hundred, a few thousand. You get comfortable with that, and before you know it, it snowballs into something big."[1] This was a comment he made when she asked him what he thought about a colleague's secretary going to prison for embezzling millions of dollars years before giving his own confession.

Hopefully, we will never see an investment scam larger than what Bernie Madoff conducted over 40 years. He made my ex-husband look like small potatoes, stealing over $50 billion dollars from investors (Brad Bleidt stole approximately $30 million and was touted at the time as being the biggest scammer since Charles Ponzi). Four years after Brad Bleidt confessed via a dramatic suicide attempt, Bernard Madoff gave in to the pressures of a market seemingly in a downward spiral that destroyed any hope that he could continue his charade. He confessed to his two sons, Mark and Andrew Madoff. Similar to my situation with my ex-husband, Mark and Andrew worked with their father, but indirectly. As far as we know now, they were not connected to their father's illegal dealings. Like Brad Bleidt, Mr. Madoff was known to be charming and innovative and influential in certain circles. Both men utilized their influence within these networks to recruit victims and feed their Ponzi schemes. They both provided their customers with consistently good performance results in both good times and bad. Clients certainly had nothing to complain about when the market was not performing well, though rates of return were not significant enough to draw suspicion or unwanted attention from skeptics or regulators. And like my ex-husband, Bernard Madoff orchestrated the events around his confession, trying to maintain control as long as possible. What is different about Bernard Madoff is that he not only took advantage of those with little experience, but also fooled the investment community. Investment

---

[1] Seal, Mark and Eleanor Squillari. (2009). "The Madoff Chronicles, Part II: What the Secretary Saw." *Vanity Fair*, 586:96.

professionals, who are supposed to be aware of custody and reporting issues, were drawn to Mr. Madoff's reputation, experience, powerful persona, and supposed success. Perhaps they were apprehensive of the consistently decent returns he produced and the minimal fees he charged for his seemed brilliance. Much about his advisory business and the techniques implemented were mysterious secrets. But Mr. Madoff had the ability to make people feel grateful for being able to do business with him. More than likely any professional fortunate enough to tap into the "Madoff magic" didn't want to rock the boat especially during and after difficult market moments. After all, investors like the idea of good and consistent returns. Many Madoff victims never even heard of the man until December of 2008 and did not learn until recently that they had lost money in the scam because they had relied on their own investment professionals who were led astray. Adding insult to injury, many of these financial professionals were well compensated for feeding clients to Mr. Madoff.

So what can we learn from the Madoff situation?

Again, we see the trend for consistently positive returns, even under difficult market conditions. There are investments out there that can provide consistent returns but not one or two percent each month as Mr. Madoff and Mr. Bleidt represented to their clients. It is for this reason investors should take the time to understand

- The investment statement
- Each individual investment
- Transaction confirmations
- Tax documents

Statements and transaction confirmations are discussed in Chapter 8, "Statements, Communications, and the 'Dreaded' Prospectus."

In the Bleidt scenario, there was no custodian for client assets. Brad Bleidt created fictitious statements on his asset management corporation's letterhead with no mention of the broker/dealer or custodian. If I had to guess, a good majority of the investing public does not understand what the various roles and relationships are of the custodian, broker/dealer, registered representative, and/or registered investment advisor. The Madoff situation is not as clear-cut as Mr. Madoff's trading firm, Bernard L. Madoff Investment Securities, LLC, was supposedly performing the account trades and acting as custodian. This is why it is important that customers understand

- Whether or not their advisors are utilizing broker/dealers and if so, with what companies are they affiliated
- What entities are the custodians of the actual assets and issuing customer statements
- Whether or not accounts are covered by the Securities Investor Protection Corporation (SIPC)
- Who the auditors for the custodians are. In the Madoff situation the firm's auditor was a three-person operation, which had been telling the American Institute of Certified Public Accountants for 15 years it was not in the business of certifying books.
- By whom the firm is being regulated: the Securities and Exchange Commission (SEC), the Financial Industry Regulatory Authority (FINRA), the State, banking authorities, and so on

While we are still learning the details of how Bernie Madoff became a scam artist instead of the successful and reputable business person that he once was, we have to wonder how it began. Did he set out with the intention of using clients' funds for his own purposes, or was it a desperate act that became a habit? His earlier successes perhaps fueled an exorbitant lifestyle that he could no longer afford once his innovative technological edge for his trading business became mainstream, though it seems the fraud started long before then. Maybe he always had a habit of living beyond his means, necessitating the support of his scam.

Certainly, like my ex-husband, Bernard Madoff is someone who is narcissistic and believes he is above "the rules." Despite his admission of guilt, he continued to live in his seven-million-dollar penthouse long after his confession. It is just so unfortunate that it took so long and so many investors financially devastated for it to catch up with him.

Like Bradford Bleidt's staff, Bernard Madoff's employees of his illegitimate investment management company apparently knew enough to help him but not enough to catch on that something wasn't right. Mr. Madoff's response to his secretary when she asked if she should go back to school to learn about finances was, "No, you don't need to do that. You've got two kids to raise. If you have to take a class, take an art class, and I'll pay for it. But not a business class."[2] At the age of 71, Bernard Madoff was sentenced to 150 years in federal prison.

QUICK TIPS

- Be sure to thoroughly check out any advisor to whom you are referred. As discussed, both Bradford Bleidt and Bernard Madoff took full advantage of their favorable positions in their respective communities—the Masons and the Jewish community.
- Verify the custodian of your invested assets. If it is not a separate entity, request information about the firm's auditor and auditing processes. Be sure also to check out the auditor.
- Understand how your invested assets will be protected. If your accounts are covered by SIPC (Securities Investor Protection Corp), verify with SIPC that the firm with which you are dealing is a member of SIPC.

---

[2] Seal and Squillari (2009).

- If your account is achieving consistent returns that are higher than what can be earned by investing in CDs and money markets, especially in times of market volatility, ask for an explanation of the investment strategy and do not settle for vague explanations.

- Understand where your money is ultimately being invested and do not accept vague answers and references to secret strategies.

- If investments are being bought and sold in your account, yet you have not received confirmation of such transactions, ask why.

- In the event your advisor is changing his or her broker/dealer affiliation, verify where your assets are going and check out the new firm. Keep in mind assets are usually transferred directly in these situations. It is highly unlikely that your advisor will return assets to you and then ask you to write a check to the new firm.

- If you are not receiving the appropriate tax documentation (1099s for regular accounts or 1099Rs for retirement distributions), verify where your assets are and how they are protected and probe into why no tax document was issued.

- Ask questions about referral arrangements. In other words, will your advisor be getting paid to invest your money with a separate investment manager? If so, request a meeting with this individual and take the proper steps to assure yourself that he, she, or the separate entity is legitimate. Though a third party money manager may not always be available to meet with you, it doesn't hurt to ask; you should collect as much information about the referral relationship as possible.

Chapter 2

What Is Financial Planning?

Financial planning is a larger field than you might think. It is actually made up of a number of components, and it is difficult for any one advisor to be an expert in every aspect of it. Relating financial planning to the medical field, you will have advisors who have a broad base of knowledge and might act as a generalist. These advisors very often can work with clients in a holistic manner but might have to find "specialists" in more complex situations. Whether you work with a generalist or a specialist, it is important to have an integrated financial plan. As one of my former colleagues put it, "If you don't know where you're going, any road will take you there." The major areas of financial planning that need to be considered are

- **Cash Flow:** This is where it all starts. Without positive cash flow, there are no funding mechanisms for other goals. Unfortunately, our culture has fostered poor cash flow habits. Americans have become far too reliant on the use of credit to feed their immediate desires to the detriment of their long-term goals. The first step to financial planning is understanding what is coming in by way of resources and what is going out via expenses and whether or not there is anything left over in the end. If the cash flow is zero or negative before other goals are funded, budgeting must be addressed.

- **Taxation:** It's not what you make; it's what you keep. Proper tax planning can actually create resources to help fund other goals. Tax laws change nearly every year, which is why it is important to review your tax return with your advisor to see if there are adjustments that can be made in order to help save money and/or fund financial planning objectives.

- **Retirement:** Financial educator Dee Lee says it in a nutshell, "There are no scholarships for retirement." For most people, retirement seems too far away when they should start saving for it that it gets put off. Throughout my 20-year career, I've seen the retirement picture change drastically. When I first started working with retirees in 1990, it was pretty typical to meet with people whose major retirement resources were Social Security and a corporate pension. Since then, I've seen more and more companies moving from Defined Benefit retirement programs to those of the Defined Contribution type. The difference? The latter puts more responsibility on the employees for decision making in regard to the vehicles for growing their retirement savings and, in many cases, funding. Though corporations do make attempts to educate their employees, efforts are not effective enough at this point and rarely impact the younger workforce. As corporate benefits change and Social Security remains in question, proper retirement planning must become a priority for the vast majority of individuals.

- **Risk Management:** This is a fancy way of saying "insurance planning." Insurance is needed for protection against those risks you can't afford to cover with your existing assets and income level. A proper financial plan will analyze what insurances are appropriate and at what levels. Coverage in the areas of life, disability, homeowners, liability, auto, and long-term care should be reviewed as part of the planning process and reviewed periodically. Coverage needs to be changed over time and is dependent on situational circumstances and financial resources.

- **Education Funding:** The cost of higher education rises each year at a rate higher than inflation; thus, it is never too early to start building a fund to cover these expenses. The problem with college funding is that it comes in direct conflict with other planning goals. For a lot of people, decisions must be made on how to allocate funds between retirement and education objectives, all the while maintaining the proper insurance coverage to protect the overall financial plan.

- **Estate Planning:** Believe it or not, everyone already has an estate plan. If you have assets, it makes sense to put some plans in for "when your case matures." (My estate planning professor, Dr. Robert C. Suter, used this phrase when referring to death.) If you have a spouse and children or elderly parents to care for, it is imperative. If your assets are above a certain level, which will vary from state to state, and you prefer to leave Uncle Sam and your state's coffers out of your will as much as possible, it is important to bring an attorney who specializes in this field onto your financial planning team.

Though not all of these areas will apply to everyone, a well-shaped plan will incorporate all applicable pieces in a way that the whole will be greater than the sum of its parts. The challenge of financial planning is one of conflicting goals. It is not atypical to have limited dollars chasing a number of different financial objectives. In this situation, planning is imperative. Plan preparation should be followed by reviews and adjustments on a regular basis. Just as most people have their health evaluated on an annual basis, financial planning should have the same prerogative. Unfortunately, most people spend more time planning their annual vacations than working on their financial futures. Hopefully, some of the positive outcomes of our most recent financial crisis are that Americans will become more responsible about spending wisely and not over using credit and learn to dedicate more time to planning their finances.

Does each area of financial planning require its own specialist? It depends on how complicated the situation is. Many financial advisers can proficiently assist clients with putting together a plan and helping them find the proper products to use and/or appropriate specialists. Unless the advisor is also an attorney, most people will need a lawyer to prepare legal documents for estate planning purposes in the client's state of residency. Some financial advisors also do tax preparation in addition to planning, though many clients choose to do their own taxes. Regardless of how many advisors are involved and what roles they play, it is important that all parties work together as a team. Frequently, the financial advisor is responsible for coordinating the various components and the individuals involved to keep the financial planning ball rolling effectively and efficiently.

In working with individuals for nearly 20 years, I've come to realize the role of various advisors can be confusing, probably because the lines are not clear cut. Typical advisors include

- **Financial Planner:** A financial planner is an advisor who is focused on the big picture and can provide direction in the various areas of financial planning. He might get paid by the hour, a set amount for a particular plan provided, based on a percentage of assets managed, and/or via product sales. In the event a planner is compensated via product sales, be sure she has the appropriate licenses and registrations for the products being provided. A financial planner can be independent or work for a brokerage firm or an insurance agency. How he has chosen to set up his practice might give you clues as to his areas of expertise and even how he gets paid. In other words, if the advisor is associated with an insurance company, she might have more of an insurance affiliation and a background in risk management and estate planning. An advisor who chooses to represent a brokerage house may be oriented toward investments. A financial planner will typically have training in the six areas of financial planning as described earlier in this chapter and is likely to have or be working toward credentials such as becoming a

CERTIFIED FINANCIAL PLANNER™ professional or Chartered Financial Consultant. Advisor designations are described in Chapter 3, "The Meaning Behind Advisor Designations and Licenses."

- **Insurance Representative:** An insurance representative might be independent and represent a number of companies or affiliated with a particular insurance company. He is likely to be compensated via the sale of products, typically insurance and annuities, though he might also be able to provide mutual funds and other investment products as well. It is important to understand whether the advisor is influenced in any way to recommend particular companies or products when providing advice or if she is able to offer a wide variety of companies and products, helping you to get the best fit for your situation. Be sure the insurance representative is licensed to do business in your state of residency as each state has its own requirements for insurance licensing. If she is also offering investments, make sure she has the proper securities licenses for the products being discussed. Licensing requirements are addressed in Chapter 3 as well.

- **Investment Representative:** Like the insurance representative, an investment professional might be independent or part of one particular company. He is likely to be compensated via product sales or assets under management. The representative is most likely to be registered with a brokerage firm or an independent broker/dealer.

- **Certified Public Accountant:** More and more CPAs and tax preparers are getting into the financial planning and investment fields. It is a natural fit given that the IRS Form 1040 and its various schedules are some of the most information-packed resources for a financial advisor. However, don't forget that it does take specialized training to provide specific recommendations on investments and insurance, not to mention proper licensing and registrations.

- **Registered Investment Advisor (RIA):** An RIA is an entity which manages money for a fee and could be regulated by the Securities and Exchange Commission or the State, regardless of whether or not it has a broker-dealer affiliation. An RIA will typically be fee-only, however some choose to affiliate with a broker/dealer so that they can also perform transactional work and get paid.

- **Investment Advisor Representative (IAR):** Performs for fee investment management services as a representative of a Registered Investment Advisor firm.

QUICK TIPS

- Grasp an understanding of the various areas of financial planning as described.
- Recognize which types of advisors might be able to help you with your own particular situation.

Chapter 3

The Meaning Behind Advisor Designations and Licenses

The more letters a financial professional has after his or her name does not necessarily correlate with the quality of the advice he or she provides. Some designations carry more clout because they require more dedication to obtain and maintain. Some are general and others specific. Depending on what your needs are, some designations and licenses will be more important to you than others. Following are some of the longest lived and more common designations you might come across and what they mean:

- **CFA—Chartered Financial Analyst:** The CFA designation is investment-oriented. A candidate must have an undergraduate degree and 3 years of professional experience involving investments or 4 years of qualified work experience. Though no course work is required, 3 full-day examinations must be passed to obtain the designation. For more information, go to www.cfainstitute.org.

- **ChFC—Chartered Financial Consultant:** A ChFC might have more of a focus in the insurance arena and is required to have 3 years of full-time business experience and pass 6 core and 2 elective courses as well as exams for each course. Thirty hours of continuing education credits are required every 2 years. For more information, go to www.theamericancollege.edu.

- **CFP® Professional:** A CFP® professional will have training in a wide range of financial planning topics and must have a minimum of a bachelor's degree and 3 years of full-time personal financial planning experience.

A candidate must also complete a CFP-board registered program consisting of at least 6 courses and pass a 2-day comprehensive exam, though certain financial professionals are exempt from the course work. CFP® professionals must complete 30 hours of continuing education courses every 2 years, including 2 hours of a qualified ethics course, and adhere to the CFP Code of Ethics and Professional Responsibility and Financial Planning Practice Standards. For more information, go to www.cfp.net.

- **CPA—Certified Public Accountant:** A CPA will have training in the area of taxation and accountancy. A bachelor's degree with relevant coursework is required as is passing the Uniform CPA Exam as well as an ethics course. CPAs can also obtain a Personal Financial Specialist designation in which case half of their 120 hours obtained within 3 years of required continuing education requirements must be financial planning-oriented. For more information, go to www.aicpa.org.

Other designations are less common but can be beneficial to the advisor in assisting you with your planning. If you are uncertain of what a particular designation means in speaking with a financial professional, ask her about it: what it means, what is involved with obtaining it, and what is required to maintain the designation in the way of continuing education requirements. You might also inquire about whether or not the issuing entity requires adherence to a code of ethics. Lesser known designations include

- **AAMS—Accredited Asset Management Specialist:** To obtain this designation, the professional must have completed a self study course, pass an examination on asset management topics, agree to a code of ethics, and commit to annual continuing education.
- **AEP—Accredited Estate Planner:** Candidates must already be a licensed attorney, CPA, CFP® professional, or

hold a CLU, ChFC, or CTFA designation. Five years of experience is required as is the completion of two specific graduate courses through the American College.

- **AIF—Accredited Investment Fiduciary:** Designees will have shown their competency in the area of fiduciary responsibility by completing a course and passing (70% or better) an exam. They must abide by a code of ethics and complete 6 hours of continuing education each year.

- **AWMA—Accredited Wealth Management Advisor:** Completion of this program helps advisors increase their knowledge in the areas of asset allocation and selection, investment strategies, and applicable taxation repercussions. Completion of a 15-module course and a proctored final exam are required along with 16 hours of continuing education every 2 years, as well as adherence to a code of ethics.

- **CAP—Chartered Advisor in Philanthropy:** Advisors with this designation have the objective of helping individuals reach their philanthropic goals, while also assisting with the noncharitable needs of estate planning and wealth management. Three years of experience is required, along with the completion of 3 self-study courses; each of which is followed by a 2-hour proctored examination. Fifteen hours of continuing education must be completed every 2 years.

- **CCPS—Certified College Planning Specialist:** Candidates must apply for approval and pass an examination. A combination of experience and education is required. Certificate holders must abide by a code of ethics and complete 24 hours of continuing education each year.

- **CDFA—Certified Divorce Financial Analyst:** (Not permitted in Nebraska.) Advisors with this designation have completed 4 self-study modules and passed an exam for each. Candidates must have 2 years of experience in the financial and/or legal fields. Fifteen hours of continuing education is required annually.

- **CEP—Certified Equity Professional:** This designation can be obtained by completing self-study courses and passing 3 exam levels. Continuing education is required.

- **CFS—Certified Fund Specialist:** Obtainment of this designation demonstrates an advisor's commitment to understanding mutual funds. He or she is able to evaluate and compare financial measurements and benchmarks of the funds when constructing a portfolio. The training is in a variety of mutual fund topics that include but are not limited to portfolio theory, dollar-cost averaging, and annuity topics. Created in 1988, CFS is the oldest designation in the mutual fund industry and is fully accredited.

- **CIC—Chartered Investment Counselor:** Professionals looking to become certified as a Chartered Financial Analyst must first be a member of the Investment Counsel Association of America (ICAA) and have 5 years of related work experience. With the completion of the requirements to get this designation, the professional will be held to a higher set of ethical standards and possess considerable experience with investment counseling and portfolio management.

- **CIMA (Formerly CIMC)—Certified Investment Management Analyst:** Individuals with 3 or more years of financial management experience who have agreed to 10 hours of continued education annually can obtain this designation. The professional must also be free of all criminal actions, regulatory violations, civil actions, and customer complaints, or present an acceptable explanation of any occurrence.

- **CLTC—Certified in Long Term Care:** Candidates must complete a 2-day course and pass a final exam. In addition, an ethics course must be taken every 2 years.

- **CLU—Chartered Life Underwriter:** A person with this designation specializes in life insurance and estate planning. Not all CLUs provide financial planning. To get this designation, professionals need to complete 8 courses and pass a final examination.

- **CMFC—Chartered Mutual Fund Counselor:** Completion of a self-study course as well as a final examination are required to obtain the CMFC. Two years of experience are a prerequisite. Sixteen hours of continuing education are required every 2 years.

- **CRC—Certified Retirement Counselor:** This designation focuses upon retirement planning and income management issues. Four self-study courses and examinations are required along with 15 hours of continuing education each year.

- **CREd—Certified Financial Educator:** Holders of this designation demonstrate knowledge and experience in teaching or instructing in the area of financial services. A course must be completed via self-study or in a classroom setting followed by a closed book exam. Designees must have 3 years of experience and complete 12 hours of continuing education each year.

- **CRPC—Chartered Retirement Planning Counselor:** This program has a focus on the pre- and post-retirement issues faced by individuals. Designees complete a self-study course and a final examination as well as 16 hours of continuing education every 2 years. Adherence to a code of ethics is also required.

- **CRPS—Chartered Retirement Plans Specialist:** Financial advisors looking to work with retirement plans for companies and small businesses are ideal candidates for this designation. The coursework required is the completion of 11 modules and passing an exam.

- **CTFA—Certified Trust and Financial Advisor:** Financial professionals with a focus on estate planning and 3 years experience in personal trusts are a good fit for this designation. The advisor must also complete an ICB trust training program or have 5 years experience in personal trusts and a bachelor's degree. Otherwise, the candidate can have 10 years of experience in personal trusts. Designees must agree to a professional code of ethics and pass an exam. Every 3 years, the designee must complete 45 hours of continuing education.

- **CWS—Certified Wealth Strategist:** Candidates must have at least 1 year of industry experience working interactively with clients. Coursework includes classroom and self-study modules, including 4 examinations. Thirty-three hours of continuing education are required each year.

- **EA—Enrolled Agent:** A federally authorized tax practitioner who has passed an examination covering the tax code or who has worked for the IRS for 5 years with tax code and tax regulations. Candidates are subject to a background check.

- **FSS—Financial Services Specialist:** This basic program provides candidates with product knowledge and sales skills. Six courses and a final exam are required.

- **LIA—Licensed Insurance Advisor:** An advisor with an insurance license.

- **LUTCF—Life Underwriter Training Counsel Fellow:** Five courses must be completed on various financial planning topics with a focus on insurance.

- **PFS—Personal Financial Specialist:** These candidates must first be CPAs and also have at least 3 years of financial planning experience. The designation is earned after passing an exam, and the board must receive positive recommendations from clients and colleagues.

- **REBC—Registered Employee Benefits Consultant:** Designees obtain an education on employee benefits including pensions, retirement, and medical plans. Five courses must be completed.

- **RFC—Registered Financial Consultant:** The candidate seeking this designation must also complete and adhere to high levels of education, experience, and integrity. There is also an exam and 40 hours of continuing education annually.

- **RP—Registered Paraplanner:** Candidates obtain basic knowledge of the 5 areas of financial planning. Ten courses must be passed as well as an examination and an internship. Sixteen hours of continuing education are required every 2 years.

Advisors may also obtain higher education degrees with a focus on various financial planning areas. It is not highly unusual to see advisors practicing who also have an MBA (Master of Business Administration), PhD (Doctorate), or JD (Juris Doctor). Master educational programs are now available at many colleges and universities in areas such as financial services, taxation, and employee benefits. Keep in mind that, although a postgraduate degree may demonstrate an individual's dedication to higher education, it may or may not provide you with any additional benefit in working with that particular advisor. Be sure to talk with any advisor candidate about the meaning behind their education and how it affects their practice.

It is also important to understand that there are over 100 financial advisor designations all with different requirements, but you can't be too careful. Some advisor designations are just "fluff" and don't mean a lot. In fact, most states are cracking down on the use of meaningless designations, especially those suggesting expertise in the areas of advising senior citizens. For more information on less commonly known designations, check out the Financial Industry Regulatory Authority's website at www.finra.org.

If your advisor is involved in the sale of products, he or she will be required to have certain licenses and be approved to sell products in your state of residency. Licenses frequently held by advisors include

- **State Insurance:** Each state has its own requirements for selling life, accident, and health insurances and annuities. Typically a licensee must pass an examination and maintain continuing education credits in his own state and apply to other states in which he wishes to do business. Go to www.naic.org for more information.

- **Series 6:** Candidates must pass a 135-minute exam that covers what are called "packaged" investments, such as mutual funds and variable annuities. The exam also covers regulations and ethics. Advisors who sell variable annuities and variable insurance must also have their insurance licenses in the states where they are providing products. Series 6 licensees are not eligible to sell other types of securities such as stocks and bonds.

- **Series 7:** Candidates must pass a six-hour exam covering most types of investments from stocks and bonds to more advanced strategies using options, and adhere to regulations and ethics. Series 7 licensees are not authorized to sell commodities futures (a Series 3 is required), real estate, or insurance without completing additional requirements. A Series 7 licensee would be referred to as a "Registered Representative" or a "stockbroker."

- **Series 24 and 26:** These are both designations of those entitled to supervise Series 6 and 7 licensees, respectively.

- **Series 63:** All Series 6 and 7 licensees must also pass the Uniform Securities Agent license required by each state.

- **Series 65:** Advisors working on a fee basis are required to pass the Series 65. This includes those working on an hourly basis and/or managing money for a fee. If the advisor is not involved with the sale of products and wants to be an Investment Advisor Representative, this is considered the state's competency examination.

- **Series 66:** A 66 candidate must have passed the Series 7 examination. The license is essentially a combination of the 63 and 65.

More information about the Series 6, 7, 24, and 26 can be found on the Financial Industry Regulatory Authority's website at www.finra.org.

More information about the Series 63, 65, and 66 can be found on the North American Securities Administrators Association's website at www.nasaa.org.

QUICK TIPS

- Recognize that all designations are not created equal.
- Clarify your own needs to match advisor experience, licenses, and designations to your own situation.

Chapter 4

Advisor Compensation

It is important to know how your financial advisor gets paid. Though good advisors are not necessarily motivated by money, they are professionals who deserve to get paid appropriately for their time. There is no free lunch. We all love getting something for nothing, but if the advisor is not taking adequate time to get to know you and your particular situation, then the free advice might actually turn out to be quite costly in the end if mistakes are made. I have seen this all too frequently. I would also have to say that most financial advisors look after their own finances pretty well. In many situations clients are unaware that they are actually getting charged because the compensation to the advisor is not totally evident. Though it may be uncomfortable, part of the process of hiring an advisor is asking how he or she is paid. The way advisors are compensated can in some instances influence their recommendations. Understanding the compensation format can help you spot abuses initially and down the road.

Here are various ways financial advisors are compensated:

- **Transactions:**   Financial advisors who are compensated via transactions get paid when you buy or sell something. They are typically insurance or investment representatives and must be licensed to sell the products they are promoting. Most advisors get paid when they sell you an A, B, or C share of a mutual fund, a variable annuity, life insurance, disability coverage, long-term care insurance or stocks, exchange traded funds, and bonds. Transactional charges are also known as *commissions*. Commission structures vary by product and can generously reward the advisor. Where a

31

potential for abuse lies is in product "replacements" or what has come to be known as "churning." If an advisor sells you a mutual fund and gets paid a commission and then a few years later wants to put you in a different mutual fund for which you will pay another commission, you might question whether the advisor is making the recommendation out of your own best interest or looking to get paid. Most mutual fund families will allow you to change funds within the same fund family without incurring additional commissions. Replacements are also known to happen in the insurance world. If an advisor is recommending you to move out of something that will cost you money to surrender in favor of a new but similar product, make sure the benefits of the new product are worth it in the end before proceeding. The word "churning" really was born out of the brokerage industry where unscrupulous traders would buy and sell securities in portfolios just to gain commissions. Though an actively traded portfolio might seem like it is being overseen by a diligent advisor looking for new opportunities, excessive trading could just be a way for the broker to make money for himself or herself and not necessarily the client.

- **Fee Only:** A fee only advisor will not get compensated by providing you product, but will charge a fee for the advice provided. He might charge you on an hourly basis, a set fee for a particular plan, and/or a percentage of your assets managed. Fee structures are generally outlined in the agreement you sign with the advisor and/or the ADV Part II. In the event the advisor will be charging by the hour, be sure to get an estimate of the hours involved in working on your case, along with the hourly rate, so you can get an idea of the ultimate cost. In an asset management situation, the advisor will get paid a percentage of what you have invested with her, usually on a quarterly basis. While this arrangement puts you on the same side of the fence as the advisor (in other words she is incentivized to grow your assets and does take a haircut when your asset level goes down), it is not completely sheltered from abuse. Be sure to understand how often your portfolio will be reviewed and how often you will interact with the advisor. Ask about how portfolios are developed and what might trigger changes in your portfolio. Also understand whether or not the advisor will have discretion (the ability to make changes in your portfolio without your authorization) or will be limited. More recently, the use of retainers has come to the financial planning world, where the client pays up front, and funds are used and accounted for over time in a similar fashion to what is done in most law firms. Advisors who are fee only do not have to have the same licenses as those who receive commissions.

- **Combination Fee and Commission:** Some advisors might have both fee-based and commissionable aspects to their practices. They may charge a fee to do a financial plan and then receive commissions for helping you implement the plan via the purchase of insurance or investment products. Others might have a commissionable "portfolio development fee" and then charge asset management fees once the assets are in place and being managed. There are various ways fees and commissions can be combined. The important thing is to understand how they are being combined in your situation and whether or not the end result is fair to you and the financial advisor. Financial professionals working in this capacity must have the appropriate registrations and licenses to be dealing with any products being recommended and sold.

- **Fee Offset:** In a fee offset situation, the advisor could be compensated via the purchase of commissionable products. If the advisor is charging you a specific fee, he might utilize commissions earned to offset the fee to be charged. Again, financial professionals working in this capacity must have the appropriate registrations and licenses to be dealing with any products being recommended and sold.

Various fee structures not only exist to accommodate different types of advisors, but also the varying situations and needs of clients. For example, a fee-structured financial plan might not be affordable for some clients without also having the option to compensate the advisor via product purchases. A wealthy client might overpay if only commissionable products are sold to him as opposed to entering into some sort of fee agreement. The goal is to understand and come to agreement about how the advisor will get adequately paid in a way that is fair to you, the customer.

QUICK TIPS

- Understand compensation structures so you can ask appropriate questions of potential advisors and assess the impact to you and your investments
- Recognize how various compensation structures can influence advisor recommendations.

Chapter 5

Deciphering Fee Structures

Portfolio Development and Asset Management

Though a thorough discussion about advisor compensation should take place before any plans are made or transactions implemented, don't just take your advisor's word for it. If your advisor is doing a financial plan for you or charging a fee to develop a portfolio, the fees should be outlined clearly for you in an agreement to be signed by both you and the advisor. Likewise, if you are paying someone a fee to manage your money, the fee structure should be spelled out via an agreement. For portfolio development and portfolio management, many advisors will have a stepped scale depending on the dollar amount of the assets being managed. Typically, the more assets being invested, the lower the fee. Portfolio development fees can be paid directly by the client, through commissionable transactions within the account, or by direction of the client to compensate the advisor through the account. More often than not, asset management fees are paid directly from the account being managed, and you should be able to see what they are and when they are paid on your account statement. Frequently, they are paid at the beginning of each quarter, so you might want to look closely at your January, April, July, and October account statements to verify the amount being paid matches that which was agreed upon.

Financial Planning

If your financial professional is doing a financial plan for you, be sure the agreement between you and the planner addresses the areas of financial planning that will be covered by the plan, such as the following:

- Cash Flow
- Taxes
- Investments
- Retirement
- Estate
- College

Also, be sure the agreement clearly spells out how much the plan will cost. Many advisors will have set fee structures for each of these areas of financial planning and/or a "comprehensive" or all-inclusive plan. Other advisors will charge by the hour. If the advisor is charging by the hour, it makes sense to get an estimate of the hours anticipated. To give a proper estimate, the planner will need to have a good overview of your finances. An agreement for a financial plan should state clearly what the planner's hourly rate is, and you might request verbiage that addresses a cap on the total investment being made. For example, "$250 per hour not to exceed ten hours or $2,500."

Stocks, Bonds, and Exchange Traded Funds

When financial advisors are compensated via product sales, their commissions might not be evident, and it is unlikely you will be signing an agreement that clearly states this information. If the financial professional is buying and selling stocks, bonds, exchange traded funds, and other individual investments, you should be provided a commission schedule. When the advisor buys or sells something, the commission will show up on what is called a "trade ticket" or *confirmation*. A confirmation goes out to the customer when a transaction is made in his account. This is true of accounts being managed for a fee as well. Thus, a customer can verify what he or she is paying, if anything, for the transaction. Any commission paid on a purchase increases your asset's cost basis for the purpose of calculating a taxable gain or loss. Similarly, a commission charged on the sale of an asset will reduce your sale proceeds.

Mutual funds, variable annuities, and variable life insurance can be a bit more complicated. When you buy these types of products, it is required by the regulatory authority (the Securities and Exchange Commission [SEC]) that you are provided with a prospectus which outlines all fees and expenses associated with that product in addition to the management of the product. Many investors don't read them because they feel they are burdensome and complicated. This is unfortunate as they do contain valuable information.

Mutual Funds

With mutual funds, the commission information is typically found within the first couple of pages. Keep in mind that "no load" or non-commissionable mutual funds do exist, and many "loaded" or commissionable funds can be purchased without commission by advisors if they are managing your money for a fee. Most mutual fund companies designate their various share classes with the letters A, B, and C:

- A shares typically provide the advisor with the most "up-front" commission or load but carry lower ongoing commission incentives or what are called *trails*. The maximum up-front charge allowed by the SEC is 8.5%, though the most expensive funds seem to cap out at around 5.75%. When you buy an A share, you will actually see that the initial value is less than what you may have initially invested. Though this can be due to market volatility, more than likely you are actually seeing the commission coming out of your investment. A shares can be sold at any time without additional cost to the client (though some mutual funds do charge a redemption fee whether they are load or no-load if the shares are sold within a certain period of time). A shares also allow for breakpoint discounts if you invest a certain dollar amount.

- B shares pay a lower commission to the advisor upon purchase but higher ongoing trails. Though you will see all of your investment going to work for you right away, the ongoing expenses will decrease your rate of return. Over time, B shares can be more expensive than A shares. B shares must be held for a certain period of time in order to avoid redemption charges or *contingent deferred sales charges (CDSC)*. The amount of these charges declines over time, dropping to zero usually in year six. At that point, most B shares do convert to the less expensive A shares. B shares costs vary by fund family, though the most expensive ones start out at around 5% CDSC.

- C shares do not cost anything up-front or upon redemption. However, they do carry higher annual expenses. Again, they can be more expensive than both A and B shares if held over time.

Mutual fund structures in regard to commissions and redemption charges will vary from fund family to fund family. Work with your advisor to understand the funds he or she is recommending and the commission structure that works best for your situation. Perhaps you prefer the A shares, knowing that in the long haul you are likely to pay fewer expenses. Maybe the B shares are attractive if you feel it is a buying opportunity and you want all of your investment to go to work right away. For some, having no up-front or redemption charges make the C shares the most attractive. There is nothing wrong with compensating your advisor through the purchase of mutual funds as long as you understand how he is incentivized and are aware of potential abuses. In fact, studies have shown that investors of "load" mutual funds tend to have higher long-term rates of return than those investing in no-load funds. Why? Some attribute the use of an advisor. But if there is excessive trading in your account where funds are moved from fund family to fund family, it is possible the advisor is more interested in her own rate of return than that of your portfolio. You should be aware that exchanges in mutual funds within the same share class of a fund family incur no new commissions. For example, if you are the owner of B shares at a particular fund company that are invested in stocks and you wish to add bonds to your portfolio, you should be able to exchange shares of your equity fund for B shares in a bond fund at the same company and maintain the same characteristics of your original investment. If you only had two years remaining of redemption fees for the equity fund, the same would apply for the new bond fund. The same applies to A shares: You would not incur a new commission for exchanging A shares for different funds at the same mutual fund company. Also don't forget about *breakpoints* if you are investing in A shares. Basically, breakpoints give you a break on the front-end load or commission if you buy over a certain dollar amount in one particular fund. Even if you don't buy all at once, under certain circumstances you can get breakpoint discounts utilizing a "letter of intent." Each fund family will have its own guidelines, but it is certainly worth looking into if you are accumulating a large amount (starting in the $25,000 range) in one particular A share fund.

Variable Annuities

Financial advisors are also required to provide prospectuses when selling variable annuities. Variable annuities are becoming more and more popular, not only for their tax deferral aspects, but also because of some of the innovative benefits insurance companies have been developing to assist in selling their products. Many are now offering principal protection and income guarantees for their investors. When the stock market is volatile, these "riders" seem pretty attractive, though they don't come without cost, of course. What you should understand about an annuity is that a) it is an insurance product, and b) it is essentially a tax-deferral wrapper. Because annuities are tax deferred vehicles already, they have come under fire in the past for being poor programs for retirement monies like IRAs and rollovers from 401(k)s. But as the insurance companies have started to focus on what are called "living benefits," they have become a good alternative in certain situations for retirement and nonretirement investments. Most variable annuities are sold in the form of B shares. In other words, all of your investment goes to work for you, but you are typically committed to that investment for a number of years, frequently seven, unless you choose to pay a redemption charge. Similar to a mutual fund, that redemption charge declines over the years you are in the contract. With many variable annuity companies, the advisor will have a choice on how he can take compensation: all up-front or some up-front with varying trail schedules. As the annuity is a wrapper, it will have a number of investment choices within the wrapper. Many of these choices (called sub-accounts) will be replicas of mutual funds that already exist. A contract will allow for a number of investment changes within the annuity wrapper per year without charge. Thus, there is no incentive for the advisor to excessively trade within a variable annuity contract. He will receive no additional compensation. Annuities can carry up-front loads or redemption charges as high as 8% or 9% and typically have fairly high internal expenses, especially when various living and/or death benefits are elected. These benefits, which offer principal guarantees during the life of the contract or upon death of the owner, add to the internal expense of the annuity contract but also bring value when the underlying investments of the program are underperforming.

Indexed Annuities

Indexed annuities are somewhat of a hybrid between fixed and variable annuities. They offer participation in market returns with the stability of providing some minimal rate of return if the contract is held for a certain period of time. Certainly, stability and guarantees are attractive features especially during times of market volatility. However, these products, along with variable annuities have come under scrutiny by regulators in regard to whether or not they are being sold appropriately. The commission incentives can be in the 9% to 10% range, so it is understandable that advisor motivation could be called into question when these products are sold. An investor should be aware of the long holding periods and high surrender charges prior to making a decision to buy an indexed annuity.

Insurance

Term life insurance, disability, and long-term care insurances are not typically considered investments, per se, though they are investments in preserving assets and income. They are pure coverage; in other words, you won't have a "cash value" with these products that will be negatively affected by any commissions paid out. An advisor providing these products is paid a commission that is normally a percentage of the cost to the customer. It can be as low as 10% and even as high as 80%, with a much lower trail being paid in subsequent years.

Fixed annuities, whole life insurance, and universal life insurance products are sometimes used as investments. Fixed products can often be a source for emergency funds. Variable accounts are often sold for funding college costs and/or retirement. Both fixed and variable programs can benefit those who need coverage but also need a way of "forced savings" since you have to pay your premiums if you want the insurance coverage. There are also ways of withdrawing funds out of insurance policies in a tax advantaged way. In general, I feel that insurance protection and investment vehicles should be kept separate. In other words, you should buy insurance to protect the risks to assets and income that you can't afford to self-insure and purchase investments to fund goals and objectives. Though I realize not everyone can afford to do both, and insurance premiums do force people to save who might not normally be disciplined enough to systematically invest. Virtually all insurance products pay whoever is selling the products a commission. Commission structures vary from product to product and company to company. With fixed and immediate annuities and whole life, you are unlikely to notice the effects of commission being paid. They tend to be in the 3% to 5% range with no continuing trail to the salesperson. A fixed annuity is much like a CD at the bank where the insurance company is making money off the spread of what they are paying you and whatever they are investing the money in elsewhere. Whole life is more complicated because of the many moving parts: premiums, interest or investment returns, mortality charges, and dividends. Universal life is actually a little easier to understand as dividend schedules don't come into play. However, you are likely to see evidence of commissions being paid via your premium payments when you get your statements. Advisors can be compensated in the 50% range of your first premium with a smaller trail in subsequent years. With most insurance products, there are holding period requirements. If you try to withdraw prior to the completion of that period, you are likely to be charged. Understand and keep a record of what the length of this time period is and the associated charges if it is not clearly illustrated for you.

QUICK TIPS

- Recognize that there are various ways that advisors can receive compensation.
- Evaluate different compensation structures to determine which is most cost-efficient for your situation.

Chapter 6

Finding Additional Fees

It is often said, "Little things mean a lot." In the case of additional fees that come as surprises to clients, I also find this saying to be quite applicable. Advisors will frequently get more caught up in "the bigger picture" and neglect to go over the smaller, sometimes annoying fees clients may come across. So, here are some additional charges you may see with various products. Keep in mind they will vary from entity to entity and product to product. The examples given are meant to give a ballpark idea and may or may not apply to your own situation.

Managed and/or Brokerage

- **Annual Maintenance:** In addition to commissions or a management fee, there might be a maintenance charge to cover expenses related to statement, tax, and other account-related communications. This will vary from firm to firm. This fee can range from $25 per year to $100+ depending on the firm and the services being rendered.

- **Closure:** If you close your account, you may be faced with a redemption fee. Again it varies from firm to firm, but it is not unusual to see fees in the area of $25–$100. If you are moving your account to a new firm, see if they will reimburse part or the entire closure fee.

- **Retirement Account:** Most retirement account custodians, whether they are mutual fund companies, brokerage firms, or banks, will charge a retirement account fee in the area of $25–$50.

- **Ticket Charge:** An administrative fee that is charged when something is bought or sold within a brokerage account. This fee will show up on your confirmation. It is not unusual to see ticket charges of $5–$30 per transaction.

- **Mailing Fee or Service Charge on Trades:** On top of the ticket charge, it is not unusual to see an additional $3–$5 administrative charge for the development and mailing of the confirmation documents.

- **Inactivity Fee:** In the event no trades occur in your account over a certain period of time, you may be charged an inactivity fee in the area of $15–$30. Either you or your broker should be notified and can take action to avoid this fee. Make sure any trades made are in your best interest and won't trigger any expensive tax consequences.

- **Margin Interest:** Interest charges that are charged in the event you borrow from your account either to invest in additional securities or for personal needs.

- **Wiring Fee:** A charge to have assets wired from one institution to another, usually in the $30 range.

- **Check/Credit Card Fees:** Additional costs associated with the presence of checking and credit card privileges associated with your brokerage account.

Variable Annuities

- **Annual Maintenance:** Typically $15–$30.

- **Mortality and Expenses:** These expenses will diminish returns but won't show up as separate items. On average, they run approximately 1%–1.2% of the contract and cover insurance, marketing, and administrative expenses of the annuity company.

- **Riders:** Many contracts offer all sorts of bells and whistles from automatic rebalancing of your portfolio, to enhanced death benefits and lifetime guarantees. While many riders might sound attractive, be aware of how the expenses will affect your investment over time. Lifetime guarantees have become very popular because of stock market volatility, but they do not come without a cost. You are essentially buying "insurance" for your portfolio. The price may be worth it in order to put your mind at ease, but do keep in mind that it's not free.

- **Surrender:** A charge that frequently starts at 7% in the first couple of years and diminishes year by year until it reaches 0% in year seven or eight.

- **Administrative and Management Fees:** Within a variable annuity, the investor has a number of "sub-accounts" from which to choose. Many of these accounts will mirror existing mutual funds. They are a package of stocks and/or bonds that are managed by a management team. The "expense ratio" gives you an idea of how much the management team gets paid and on average is approximately 1.2%. This expense ratio can be lower for bond sub-accounts and higher for international and small cap sub-accounts.

Mutual Funds

- **Administrative and Management Fees:** Similar to the variable annuity investor, the mutual fund investor should be aware that expense ratios exist in the same fashion for mutual funds and can diminish the overall rate of return.

- **12B-1 Fees:** These are actually fees charged by the fund company for marketing and share holder services. Charges can run from 0% to 1%.

- **Redemption Fees:** Fees charged upon the redemption of a mutual fund. Some fund families have implemented the fees to prevent attempts by investors to actively trade their mutual funds. The maximum redemption fee (which is different than a contingent deferred sales charge or closure fee) that a fund can charge is 2%. Some fund families impose this redemption charge for six months or a year after purchasing a fund; others in rare cases maintain it indefinitely.

Exchange Traded Funds and Index Funds

- **Administrative and Management Fees:** ETFs and index funds are similar to mutual funds and variable annuity sub-accounts in that they are packages of many stocks and/or bonds or other securities. The difference is that they are considered "passively" as opposed to "actively" managed. In other words, they will follow an equity, fixed income, or other index. For this reason they carry much lower expense ratios, typically 0.15%–0.25%. However, if they are bought and sold as part of a brokerage account, some of these other referenced fees may apply. Because ETFs trade like stocks, advisors can earn commissions on them when traded.

QUICK TIPS

- Recognize that in addition to advisor compensation, you might encounter additional charges.
- Get a good handle on what additional charges there may be and what impact they can have on you and your investments.

Chapter 7

Financial Products and Advisor Compensation

Some clients are unaware that financial advisors do sometimes get paid by issuers of the products they sell, and many don't realize just how much some sales can generate. The vast majority of advisors do get paid, though many participate in volunteer work from time to time, whether it is through a formal program or just helping out people here and there. Regardless, when you work with an advisor, do be prepared that they need to get paid, and you should be clear about how they are compensated. Many advisors will offer a free initial meeting for the purpose of you getting to know them and them getting to know you and to see if there is the potential of a working relationship. It is through this process that questions regarding compensation should be addressed before any real work is done. Also know that the better prepared you are for such a meeting, the more you are likely to get out of it.

As discussed previously, advisors who work on a transactional basis get paid when financial products are brought and sold. Through the transactions, they are paid commissions. These products are what are called *loaded products* and can include insurance, annuities, and mutual funds. Stocks, bonds, and exchange traded funds can be marked up when purchased or marked down when sold in order to compensate the broker. Annuities, mutual funds, stocks, bonds, and exchange traded funds can be transacted on a noncommissionable basis, though insurance typically pays the advisor a commission that might or might not be evident. With some purchases or sales it will be readily apparent what came out of your investment. Keep in mind that not all of that will go to your financial professional. Likely, the insurance company, brokerage house, or broker/dealer will keep a portion of it depending on the entity, product, and possibly your financial representative's own level of "production" with the company with whom he has aligned himself. Compensation schedules vary greatly depending on what your needs are, where you are receiving services and from company to company and advisor to advisor. So you don't suffer sticker shock when speaking with advisor interviewees, the following are some possible ranges of fees and commissions you might come across when dealing with various financial products and services:

Investment-Related

- **Portfolio Development:** Approximately 1%–3%. This fee would be paid through commissions earned on transactions or as a separate payment. It is also a tax deductible item if it is paid via a separate payment and not through commissions.

- **Asset Management:** Depending on the level of assets being managed, the fee can be in the area of 1%–3%. These fees are typically paid out of the accounts being managed and are tax deductible as long as they are not paid out of a retirement account.

- **Traded Securities (i.e., stocks, bonds, exchange traded funds):** As little as five dollars to approximately 2% if working with a full service broker. Commissions are not generally tax deductible as they are added to the tax basis or cost of a purchase of securities and lower the sales proceeds of a sales transaction reducing any taxable capital gain. A taxable capital gain is calculated by subtracting the total purchase price from the total sales proceeds; thus, commissions paid reduce the amount that is taxable.

- **Variable Annuities:** 0%–7%. Though the broker selling you the product is most likely compensated by a variable annuity transaction, commissions earned will not show up as a charge to you; rather, they are accommodated via the annual expenses of the contract.

- **Fixed Annuities:** 0%–6%. Like the variable contract, you don't see the commissions charged to your account, but they may be reflected in your surrender value.

Insurance Coverage

Insurance pays a high percentage of the premium amount in commission to the agent or broker when the product is sold and a lower percentage amount in subsequent years. The purpose of the "trail" is to compensate the individual for servicing your insurance program, so you should never feel bad about calling this individual for help with your contract. Some "no-load" options for insurance are starting to emerge.

- **Whole Life:** 50%–80% of the initial premium followed by approximately 5% of the subsequent years' premiums.
- **Variable Life:** 50%–80% of the initial premium followed by approximately 5% of the subsequent years' premiums.
- **Universal Life:** 50%–80% of the initial premium followed by approximately 5% of the subsequent years' premiums (there are some limitations on commissions depending on how much premium is placed in a universal life contract as it is sometimes used as a tax shelter).
- **Term:** 0%–70% of the initial premium followed by approximately 5%–10% of the subsequent years' premiums.
- **Disability:** 40%–50% of the initial premium followed by approximately 10% of the subsequent years' premiums.
- **Long-Term Care:** 40%–50% of the initial premium followed by approximately 10% of the subsequent years' premiums.

Financial Planning

- **Comprehensive Financial Plan:** $1,000–$10,000+ depending on the complexity of the plan as well as the location and experience of the advisor.

- **Hourly Consultation:** $100 to $400 per hour depending on location of advisor, type of counsel being provided, and the expertise and experience of the individual providing advice. Keep in mind that a higher priced advisor with more experience might actually be able to provide information more efficiently, thus keeping your overall costs lower than someone with less experience charging lower rates.

- **Retainer:** $1,000 plus depending on the assets being managed as well as their value, the complexity of planning that needs to be done, and the location and experience of the advisor.

QUICK TIPS

- Consider the total possible compensation for a potential advisor between fees and commissions.
- Recognize how various products' compensation schedules could influence advisor recommendations.

Chapter 8

Statements, Communications, and the "Dreaded" Prospectus

Whoever said we would become a paperless society was mistaken when it comes to the financial industry. Though online access has evolved, and many firms are moving toward *e-statements* for regulatory reasons, the financial industry is far from paperless. Clients can frequently be inundated and overwhelmed with what arrives in their mailboxes—much of it thrown out, unread. Investors receive statements for each account, usually on a monthly basis, annual reports, prospectuses, proxies, and so on. As one of my clients lamented to me one time, "I feel sorry for my mail carrier." I also find many of my client review meetings begin with a mail sorting session and a discussion about what to keep and what to throw out.

Statements

Whether you invest through a brokerage firm or directly with a mutual fund or variable annuity company, you should be receiving statements on a quarterly basis at minimum. Mutual fund companies and variable annuity companies generally provide reporting of assets and transactions to clients on a quarterly basis. Brokerage firms tend to send out statements monthly, though many have gone to quarterly reporting if an account has had no activity. If your assets are being actively managed, in other words you are paying a fee for someone to manage the account, you are likely to receive an additional statement on a quarterly basis. This is typically a statement that will show not only positions and activity, but also provide performance reporting for the assets and portfolio as a whole.

When reviewing your statement, whether it is of the monthly or quarterly variety, compare the latest month's positions with those of the previous month. Has anything changed? Have the number of shares in any one position gone up or gone down? If so, do you understand why? Was something sold, or was there some form of distribution that was reinvested? If so, such a transaction should show up in the activity section of the report. In the event that something was bought or sold, did you receive a separate confirmation statement from the custodian of the account? If everything matches up appropriately, the old statement can go into the shredder, though I do recommend clients hold on to year end reports for reference reasons. However, be careful of destroying records that contain important "cost basis" information. Though most fund companies and brokerage custodians do maintain this information for customers, as far as the IRS is concerned, it is each individual's responsibility to keep track of capital gains and losses. Asset sale information is reported to the IRS; thus, cost information needs to be reported by the taxpayer in order to avoid paying taxes on the entire proceeds of a sale. And though most firms will transfer this information should you move your assets from one company to another, you need to verify that this is, in fact, being done for you, or you could run into some research headaches down the road. This becomes especially tricky if you are reinvesting dividends and capital gains. Record keeping for investments within IRAs and other tax deferred vehicle shells, such as variable annuities, is not necessary from a tax standpoint as pretax contributions and any growth are drawn out from these vehicles as "ordinary income" and taxed as such. What you must keep track of with tax deferred accounts are any contributions made with monies on which you already paid taxes. Holding onto any statements with this type of information could be useful to avoid double taxation and for reporting ordinary losses in some situations. Many firms do keep statement copies on line, but be aware that it is not unusual for companies to charge for copies or for any research that needs to be done to locate particular information.

Prospectuses—Mutual and Exchange Traded Funds

An investment prospectus, as complicated and intimidating as it may be, is an excellent source of information regarding investments you are considering buying or that a broker may be buying for you. A prospectus is provided before or at the time an investment is made. Thus, in many cases, you are likely to end up with not one, but two prospectuses: one at the time the investment is discussed and another when the transaction is made. Even though most mutual fund and exchange traded fund prospectuses are available online these days, you should still expect to receive one in the mail when an investment is made. New prospectuses are issued when changes are made to the fund, and updated ones are typically provided on an annual basis. Though most investors choose to file these booklets in the trash compactor, it makes sense to keep a file of current investments you own. When an updated prospectus is issued, review it for any relevant changes, and replace the out-of-date one. If a security in your portfolio has been sold, it might make sense to then also get rid of the applicable prospectus. And yes, prospectuses do not make great reading material unless you are having difficulty sleeping, but they do contain important information. Here are a few things to look for when reviewing a prospectus:

- **Date:** Fund companies are required to update their prospectuses every 13 months. Thus, you should be sure you are in possession of one that is up to date especially if you are making an initial purchase.

- **Investment Objective:** The fund's investment objective is stated at the beginning of the prospectus. Be sure the objective is one that is appropriate for your own portfolio. Pay particular attention to the section describing "risks."

- **Performance:** The prospectus is required to present returns for the past ten years or the life of the fund, whichever is longer. Pay particular attention to the down years and translate the percentages to actual dollar amounts. If you had $30,000 invested and the fund you purchased dropped by 30% or more, as many did in 2008–2009, how comfortable would you be seeing your investment decline by $10,000 or more? The performance pages also show you how the fund performed relative to a market index, such as the S&P 500 as well as an idea of how performance could be affected by taxes. This data is not pertinent if you are holding the fund in a tax deferred account like an IRA, but it is very important if you are holding it in a taxable account. After all, it's not what you make but what you keep!

- **Fees and Expenses:** Speaking of "what you keep," the beginning of the prospectus also summarizes fee and expense information. It is here you can see the difference in the fees for the various share classes. The information summarizes the various loads, deferred sales charges, redemption fees, management costs, distribution or 12B-1 fees, and any other costs affecting the different share classes.

- **Shareholder Information:** This section includes information about buying, selling, and exchanging fund shares whether or not there are any required minimums or excessive trading policies. It also goes over options for dividends and capital gains as well as tax information.

- **Financial Highlights:** The highlight section is typically at the back of the prospectus and will generally include income and expense data on a per-share basis. The section also covers expense and portfolio turnover ratios. Turnover ratios are not always an indication of tax efficiency, but higher turnover ratios indicate more security sales within the portfolio that could end up as a taxable distribution.

Though the prospectus may seem intimidating, it is worth looking through. There is a lot of valuable information presented. The more you get used to looking through the prospectus, the more value it will bring in understanding the investments you own and those you are considering in the future. Many fund companies prepare a combination prospectus. In other words, multiple funds are represented in one prospectus booklet. Be sure the information you are reviewing pertains to only the fund or funds you own.

Shareholder Updates and Annual Reports

Mutual fund investors, in addition to receiving an updated prospectus each year, may also receive annual reports and updates from fund families with which they are invested. These reports provide the investor with information regarding the fund's performance and might offer incite into how the fund did relative to a relevant market index. In other words, a large cap U.S. stock fund might be compared with the S&P 500 index. These reports describe the fund's results and general market conditions provided by the management team. They also contain long-term performance tracking and information about sales charges as well as expenses. The portfolio of the mutual fund is included describing what securities are held, how many shares, and the values as of the date of the report. These updates provide asset and liability as well as operations statements, and a report from the fund's independent accounting firm identifying that entity. The fund's trustees, officers, and custodian are also identified along with proxy voting results, policies, and information. Tax information is made available as well along with the fund's contact information.

These reports are intimidating in appearance, but they do contain useful information to help investors understand the fund in which they are investing.

Prospectuses—Variable Annuities

Like a fund prospectus, the variable annuity prospectus provides a lot of valuable information on fees and expenses, risks, and sub-account performance. Unlike mutual funds and exchange traded funds, variable annuities have evolved to include all sorts of automatic and elective living and death benefit riders. Thus, a variable annuity prospectus contains a lot more information to digest, and sometimes it is difficult to discern what information is applicable to the variable annuity you are buying. It is for this reason you should be clear on the benefits being presented to you so that you can more easily isolate the parts of the prospectus that pertain to you and your purchase.

Because a variable annuity can be considered a tax deferred "shell," which encompasses chosen sub-accounts, you not only need to learn about the sub-accounts in which you are investing, but the "shell" contract as well. Though many of the available contract provisions sound good, additions can make annual costs for a variable annuity sky rocket, so you should be careful with your choices.

Standard Charges (on Most Contracts)

- **Mortality and Expense Risk:** A fee charged by the insurance company to protect itself from the various risks associated with issuing contracts to customers with varying circumstances. It is sometimes used to pay the selling costs (commission) of the product and is typically expressed as a percentage of the contract value.

- **Administrative Charges:**   Charges by the insurance company to cover its administrative expenses in regard to the contract, expressed as a percentage of the contract value.

- **Annual Fee:**   Another way for an insurance company to cover its administrative and record keeping expenses, typically expressed as a flat fee.

- **Surrender Charges:**   Most contracts do not carry "up-front" charges that can reduce the initial investment amount; rather, they carry "surrender" charges that reduce the "surrender value" of the contract.

- **Sub-Account Expenses:**   Because sub-accounts are similar to mutual funds, they will have an *expense ratio*, which affects your rate of return. Typically they are higher for equity sub-accounts, especially international and small-cap fund replicas, and lower for fixed income sub-accounts.

- **Investment Change Fees:**   Most contracts allow for a certain number of sub-account switches each year before a charge is assessed.

Rider Electives

- **Living Benefits:**   Include principal, growth, and/or income "guarantees," "bonus" benefits (contracts that provide you a bonus or a percentage of your investment upon signing up), and shortened or no surrender charge options.

- **Death Benefits:**   Provide contract valuation guarantees upon your death.

Proxy Materials

If you are a shareholder of individual company stock, you are likely to receive notification of the company's annual meeting along with an annual report and voting proxy information. If you have never attended an annual meeting and you have the opportunity and it is convenient, it might make sense to attend just for the experience. The annual report identifies the board of directors and senior management individuals of the corporation. It talks about the business and stockholder matters, provides financial statements, as well as information on corporate governance, executive compensation, security ownership, and transactions. The proxy card contains voting instructions along with a return envelope. Voting items can include board positions, compensation matters, and independent auditor appointments.

QUICK TIPS

- Review monthly and quarterly statements in comparison to the prior statement.
- Match up any buying or selling activity with separate confirmations issued by the custodian.
- Keep records reporting
  - After tax contributions.
  - Asset purchases.
- Hold on to year-end statements.
- Review most recent prospectuses for fee and expense information.
- When throwing out items, shred documents with references to account numbers and other identifying features rather than simply throwing them away to protect yourself from identity theft.

Chapter 9

The Roles of Various Financial Institutions

When you engage with a financial advisor, you are not only entering into a relationship with that individual and his or her staff, but also creating connections to various financial institutions. How simple or complex the web of connections depends on any products with which the advisor furnishes you and what services he will be performing. Understanding the various roles of financial institutions and how they are associated with different products and services can give you clues as to whether or not you are receiving the appropriate communications and help you spot red flags should they pop up. For example, it is my understanding that my ex-husband in certain circumstances was furnishing particular clients with immediate annuities for the purposes of doing Medicaid planning for clients in or about to enter nursing homes. An immediate annuity turns a lump sum into an income stream, similar to a pension, and in most cases the investment is irrevocable; in other words, you can't get it back after a free look period, making it difficult for the state to attach the asset for the repayment of Medicaid funds. Of course the state can, under many circumstances, attach the income stream and any remainder depending on the situation. Many immediate annuities end upon the death of the person receiving the income, allowing the insurance company to benefit in the event the individual did not live beyond their life expectancy. I suppose my ex-husband could have viewed this type of business as the perfect addition to his Ponzi scheme given that these individuals were likely ill, and he would have benefited by not having had to return a lump sum as long as he managed to pay out the "contractual" income. The fact is, an immediate annuity is issued by an insurance company in most cases. Thus, an individual purchasing an immediate annuity would not only receive the contractual periodic income distribution, but he would also be issued a policy. Of course, it is extremely easy these days for a deceptive individual to create a valid looking immediate annuity contract in exchange for a lump sum. However, any policy would contain the name of the issuing insurance company and a policy number assigned to the contract. It would be quite simple to verify that a valid immediate annuity had been purchased for the lump sum agreed upon by calling the issuing company and giving them the contract number. In addition, any checks or direct deposits would also come from the same insurance company, not from the financial professional who sold the contract.

So who are the various financial institutions who support services and products furnished by financial professionals? Again it depends on the types of products and/or services you need. In the event you are working with an advisor for the pure purpose of doing financial planning, there may or may not be a financial institution playing a supporting role. If you pay someone by the hour or for a particular type of financial plan and make no investment, you will receive a financial planning document describing your current situation, where it is you want to go, and an outline of how to get there. All fees and services to be provided will be outlined in an engagement letter that you complete prior to paying any fees or any work getting done. The final plan document product will either be acceptable to you or not. The only funds you have at risk are the fees that you pay for the preparation of the financial plan document. It is when some sort of investment is being made—whether it is to purchase investments or an insurance policy—that it makes sense to verify that your assets end up exactly where you've been told they are going.

Investments in Insurance Products

Whether you are buying variable, whole life, or term insurance or investing in variable or fixed deferred or immediate annuities, some sort of policy or certificate will be issued after an application has been completed and a deposit made. The insurance company will provide you with a "free look" period so that you may review the contract. The name of the insurance carrier and your policy number will be on this document. A call to the carrier to confirm this information is, unfortunately, not a bad idea in this day and age. There are two types of insurance companies. A *mutual insurance company* is one that is not publicly traded but instead "owned" by the policy holders. It is the policy holders who elect the board of directors for the company. Policy holders can also receive dividends or premium refunds in the event risk expenses are better than expected. A *stock insurance company* is owned by the shareholders. With both types of companies, how your premiums are invested depends on the products you purchase.

With whole and universal life insurance and fixed and immediate annuities, your premiums get invested with the insurance company with whom you are doing business. The cash values attributed to a whole life insurance policy can accumulate over time depending on excess premiums being paid and dividend schedules. For fixed annuities, the investment attributed to the contract will earn interest while invested, though that interest is likely to vary over time depending on what interest rates in general are doing. With immediate annuities, the interest rate is typically "locked in" at the time of purchase. Universal life insurance policies also earn interest on the premiums credited. The interest rate can change over time. The growth of the cash value is dependent on the premiums being paid plus the interest, minus the mortality charges and expenses. If the expenses are larger than the premiums and interest being paid, the policy will eventually lapse.

Variable life and annuity policy performance is dictated by the investments chosen as part of the plan. Variable programs will have a variety of equity and fixed income sub-accounts into which the policy owner can choose to invest premium payments. Poor performance of the elected sub-accounts can lead to inferior policy performance and potentially a policy lapse.

With any insurance-based program it is important to understand the financial stability of the insurance company. Stock insurance companies may provide for more transparency as they are publicly traded. However, given much of the recent turmoil financial companies have experienced, both stock and mutual insurance companies seem to be willing to provide information about financial stability to existing and potential customers. Though the ratings agencies have been criticized during the latest financial crises, they are a source of information and may be a place to start. The major agencies are Standard & Poor's, Moody's, A.M. Best, and Fitch. These agencies assign letter grades to financial institutions. Through their reports a potential policy purchaser can get an idea of where their possible insurers stand and whether or not their financial grades are going up or down. Some of the criticism that emerged during the latest financial crisis is that these agencies are too slow to change ratings, cozy with corporate management, and have not fully recognized the risks associated with evolving financial products. As I well know, what doesn't kill you makes you stronger. Let's hope this most recent crises and the resulting criticism will mean more accurate ratings information in the future. Additional information about the major ratings agencies is provided in Appendix A, "Consumer Resources."

In addition to accessing the information provided by the various ratings agencies, request financial quality information from the advisor who is recommending the insurance products to you. Even though insurance programs are backed by state-based protection, which is sponsored by a conglomerate of insurance companies in the event an

THE ROLES OF VARIOUS FINANCIAL INSTITUTIONS

insurance carrier fails, they are not protected by the Federal Deposit Insurance Corporation (FDIC) or the Securities Investor Protection Corporation (SIPC). In addition, policy owners sometimes have difficulty having immediate access to their funds.

Investment Management and Investment Product Sales

If you are utilizing an advisor to make investments for you and/or to manage your money, in most cases, you will not make a check payable to that individual. Getting a handle on the various entities involved with the advisor and his role will not only help you protect yourself but also provide valuable understanding about the various communications you will receive once you invest your capital.

The Broker/Dealer

If the financial professional with whom you are doing business is compensated via investment product sales—in other words, she receives commissions when buying and sometimes selling investment products for clients—she needs to be registered with a broker/dealer. The broker/dealer is often referred to as the "home office" in that many of the entities have evolved to provide registered representatives with much more than a trading platform to buy and sell securities. Most broker/dealers now provide compliance, marketing services, practice management support, training, and education for their representatives and their staff members. And why wouldn't they? The broker/dealer is responsible for compensating the registered representative with the commissions he or she earns. But, of course, the broker/dealer also must get paid and typically does via a percentage of the financial professional's earnings. Broker/dealers are regulated by the Securities and Exchange Commission (SEC) as well as the

Financial Industry Regulatory Authority (FINRA). The broker/dealer is responsible for overseeing the registered representatives affiliated with the organization; thus, a lot of attention is paid to the area of compliance. In addition to having trade requests supervised, registered representatives must have correspondences (regular mail and electronic communication) monitored and their advertising approved, including mass mailings. They must also abide by continuing education requirements, keep the broker/dealer up to date on any "outside business activities," receive approval for such activities, answer compliance questionnaires, and be subjected to audits by the broker/dealer. While this seems like a lot of supervision, unfortunately holes still exist. In my ex-husband's case, his activities were intentionally hidden from the auditors representing the SEC, NASD (now FINRA), and the various broker/dealers with whom he did business. Though steps have been taken since then to fill detection gaps, clever crooks are constantly looking for new ways to take advantage of cracks in the system. It is for this reason that it is critical to understand where your money is and who has access to it.

The Custodian

Though the broker/dealer can execute customer trades and direct funds to be sent upon client request, the entity does not actually have physical possession of the funds. This responsibility is that of the *custodian*. The custodian has actual custody of the assets in the brokerage account. Some examples of custodians include Schwab, TD Ameritrade, JP Morgan, and Fidelity. It is through the custodian that brokerage accounts are provided with protection against firm failure via the SIPC and possibly additional insurance. The custodian is also the entity that issues the brokerage statements and any tax reporting documents. Though a brokerage statement will have the name of the registered representative and the broker/dealer if applicable on it, the issuer is the custodian.

If the financial advisor with whom you are working is a Registered Investment Advisor (RIA) or Investment Advisor Representative (IAR) and working with you on a fee only basis, it is possible that there will be no broker/dealer relationship. RIAs and IARs do not have to register with a broker/dealer because they work on a fee only basis and do not sell products, though many also choose to do commission business and maintain a broker/dealer relationship. An RIA is required to register with the Securities and Exchange Commission if the advisor has $100 million dollars under management or more. Smaller RIAs register with state securities authorities and are regulated by the individual state regulators.

The Federal Deposit Insurance Company

Many investors are familiar with the FDIC through their banking relationships, though many do not realize this type of coverage does not extend to other depositor type relationships. The FDIC insurance is funded by the banking industry and covers deposits in banks and thrift organizations. Though these types of institutions may have representatives who can sell annuities, life insurance, mutual funds, Treasury securities, and/or managed accounts, the FDIC coverage does not extend to these types of investments. The FDIC insurance covers savings, checking, CDs, insured money market deposits, retirement, and trust accounts through a banking relationship. Deposits were insured up to $250,000 per depositor through the end of 2009. At that time, the insured amount returned to $100,000 per social security number, though certain retirement accounts will continue to provide the higher insurance limit. You should also be aware that the Federal Deposit Insurance Company does not protect the contents of your safe deposit box either. For more information the FDIC has provided helpful information on their website at www.fdic.gov. They can also be contacted by telephone at (877) ASK-FDIC or (877) 275-3342.

The Securities Investment Protection Corporation (SIPC)

Many investors believe that coverage provided by the SIPC is similar to that of the FDIC but meant for brokerage customers. SIPC coverage is actually quite different, and it is important to understand how it protects customers. Most brokerage customers invest in assets with constantly changing valuations. It should be understood by investors of these assets that values can go up and they can go down— sometimes quite quickly! It is for this reason the SIPC cannot possibly insure brokerage customers' deposits. How it protects customers is by stepping in when a firm fails and investor assets are missing. The coverage provided by the SIPC is $500,000 per customer including $100,000 for cash. Custodians may also provide insurance coverage, which supplements the SIPC program. When working with an advisor, be sure to understand who the custodian of your assets will be and verify that SIPC coverage exists for your accounts. "Member SIPC" will be on literature provided by the broker-dealer or custodian. Should you have doubts, you can contact the Securities Investment Protection Corporation for confirmation via their website at www.SIPC.org or contact their membership department at (202) 371-8300.

QUICK TIPS

- Verify where your investments are going.
- Determine how your funds are protected.

Chapter 10

Understanding What You Need

Like doctors, there are a lot of different types of financial advisors out there. Typical areas of expertise and the planning that can be incorporated, depending on your situation, include

- **Tax Planning:** Analysis of the existing tax situation, proper preparation of tax documents, and implementation of income tax liability reduction techniques leading to increased cash flow. Tax laws change nearly every year; thus, planning should be reviewed regularly.

- **Estate Planning:** Preparation for the preservation and efficient transfer of assets to the next generation and/or beneficial entities, including charitable. Estate settlement can be quite expensive when no plan is in place because of the expenses of probate and potential estate and/or inheritance taxes that can come into play on both the federal and state levels. Estates not taxed federally can be impacted by hefty state inheritance or estate taxes. What's more, assets can end up in the wrong hands if no planning is done. Plan development and execution will typically require the involvement of an attorney, if the advisor is not a member of the legal profession, to prepare legal documents. Typical documents most people should execute and keep up to date include the will (directs how and to whom assets should be transferred), healthcare directives (appoints individuals to make healthcare decisions in the event of incapacitation), and power of attorney (appoints individuals to make business decisions in the event of incapacitation). The more complex a situation is, often the more planning is required.

- **Investment Strategy:**   Review of existing assets, how they are held and invested, development of goals and objectives, as well as an investment policy statement, asset allocation development, and asset selection and possibly implementation and continuous monitoring of the resulting portfolio.

- **Cash Flow and Budgeting:**   Analysis of existing sources of income and spending habits most needed in cases of negative cash flow, increasing debt balances and declining or stagnant net worth growth. Many individuals ignore the problem of negative cash flow and wait too long to get help, digging themselves into holes they can't get out of. A regular cash flow check, either self-performed or with the assistance of an advisor, can prevent bigger problems down the road. An advisor focused in this area can help restructure debt to reduce interest rates and potentially payments, as well as recommend reasonable spending goals. Successful budgeting does, however, require discipline by the individual once an advisor has assisted in putting plans together.

- **Retirement:**   Determination of the future cost of retirement based on desired spending, understanding of existing and potential resources (pension, Social Security), development of a savings plan road map based on time frame, risk tolerance, and incorporation of other goals, such as college funding. Proper retirement planning requires an understanding of the existing tax situation and what it is likely to be at the time of retirement in order to determine what types of savings vehicles might work best and complement the existing tax environment.

- **Risk Management (Insurance):**   Analysis of existing vulnerabilities to personal liability and loss as well as existing assets and protective programs already in place to discover gaps where coverage is needed or where excesses exist. Risk management planning also means understanding your existing resources, what risks you can afford to cover yourself,

UNDERSTANDING WHAT YOU NEED

and insuring those areas that could create financial hazards. Resulting recommendations might be to alter or purchase additional automobile, homeowners, umbrella, health, disability, life, and/or long-term care insurance coverage.

- **College Funding:** Understanding the future cost of potential higher learning institutions as well as existing resources and potential support programs. College costs continue to rise at a rate higher than inflation; thus, planning should begin as soon as possible. Savings vehicles for the particular purpose of education funding have been developed, such as the 529 Plan and the Coverdell Education Savings Account (ESA) or Education IRA to help with the tax efficient savings of education funds. However, existence of these accounts can affect potential financial aid resource availability in the future. Thus, it is important to develop a strategy that will maximize all available resources.

Though many advisors have general knowledge in most financial planning areas, they tend to spend more time working in some areas than others, depending on how their practices have evolved over time and where their own interests lie. Most people have planning needs in each of these areas, as well. After all, we all need to manage cash flow effectively to get by. Most of us are subject to income taxation, must plan for our retirements, protect ourselves along the way, and have a desire to direct our accumulations once our "cases mature." Financial planning should be approached in a holistic manner. Each of these areas affects the others: a focus on college funding could jeopardize a balanced budget, or poor retirement income planning could produce an unreasonable tax bill. An effective and efficient financial plan will emphasize those planning aspects that cooperate, such as decreasing taxes to increase cash flow, and coordinate those that conflict in the way retirement and education planning do. Financial planning itself is in conflict with financial goals as it can be somewhat costly. It is worth the investment and typically pays for itself over time by bringing balance and financial efficiency into the picture. It is for these reasons that you do want to work with someone with expertise in the area where you need to focus but who will also pay attention to any implications recommended adjustments could cause to the big picture.

Financial planning means making priorities. Many people have too few dollars chasing expensive financial goals. A good advisor will help you understand the price tags associated with various goals and help you make savings priorities. An efficient financial plan is one where the whole is greater than the sum of its parts and each of those parts are working together like a well-oiled machine. Of course, there will be disruptions to the plan over time, which is why it is important to periodically review the plan, especially during periods of change. The overall plan should have a "check up" on its financial health once a year just as many of us do for our physical health on an annual basis. I find tax time is a good time of year to do this because financial records are pulled together for purposes of income tax return preparation. It is a good time to do a quick net worth check (how much you own minus how much you owe) and compare it to the year prior. It is certainly a good sign if it is increasing as long as it is growing as fast as you need it to in order to meet your financial goals. If the net worth is *decreasing* or not growing adequately, it's time to evaluate why. Is it because of a bad year for the financial markets? Was there a change in income resources? Was there a large expenditure during the year either anticipated or not? If it was unexpected, this might be an indication of gaps in your risk management planning. Perhaps the decline is due to poor cash management, in which case you need to address the situation and get it in line before spending gets out of control.

The need for financial planning or a revisit to an existing plan can also be influenced by life changes and circumstances; providential, emotionally neutral, unfortunate, and tragic. In my own situation, I was forced to reevaluate my entire financial picture and plans when my then husband blew up everything in my life (and those of so many others) with his dramatic confession. As with many of life's curve balls, it took years to sort out, and I continue to be affected by what he did even now, five years later. As with many situational changes, it has required a lot of patience and the need to keep my emotions in check. Emotions sometimes work against us in choosing and maintaining a proper course. A good financial advisor addresses change from a non-emotional viewpoint and steers his or her clients down a logical path.

Proper planning can be protective against change, but it is most likely that your financial setup will have the need for a review when life sends you on a detour, big or small, or you could end up getting lost! Whether you have been working with an advisor or not, times you should take a nonemotional look at your financial situation and whether or not it needs alterations include:

- **Tax Planning:**   Marriage, divorce, birth or loss of a child, new job or loss of a job, inheritance, employer benefit changes, disability, uninsured loss or liability, tax law changes, market volatility, and portfolio adjustments

- **Estate Planning:**   Marriage, divorce, birth or loss of a child, new job or loss of a job, inheritance, employer benefit changes, disability, uninsured loss or liability, and estate tax law changes

- **Investment Strategy:**   Marriage, divorce, birth or loss of a child, new job or loss of a job, inheritance, employer benefit changes, disability, uninsured loss or liability, tax law changes, market volatility, and cyclical changes in the economy

- **Tax Planning:**   Marriage, divorce, birth or loss of a child, new job or loss of a job, inheritance, employer benefit changes, disability, uninsured loss or liability, tax law changes, and market volatility

- **Cash Flow and Budgeting:**   Marriage, divorce, birth or loss of a child, new job or loss of a job, inheritance, employer benefit changes, disability, uninsured loss or liability, tax law changes, and market volatility
- **Retirement:**   Marriage, divorce, birth or loss of a child, new job or loss of a job, inheritance, employer benefit changes, disability, uninsured loss or liability, tax law changes, and market volatility
- **Risk Management (Insurance):**   Marriage, divorce, birth or loss of a child, new job or loss of a job, inheritance, employer benefit changes, disability, uninsured loss or liability, and market volatility
- **College Funding:**   Marriage, divorce, birth or loss of a child, new job or loss of a job, inheritance, employer benefit changes, disability, uninsured loss or liability, tax law changes, and market volatility

As you can see, all of these areas of financial planning intersect and overlap in various ways. It is for this reason each area needs to be addressed in conjunction with any affects on or influences by the other components of an efficient financial plan.

To better understand what you need out of a financial advisor, you may want to prepare two very basic accounting worksheets: the income statement and the balance sheet. I know for anyone who's ever taken any sort of accounting class in high school or college the thought of preparing these documents can cause you to cringe. But it's not that bad, really! What's more is the preparation of these statements will make you better prepared to meet and interview a financial professional. A trained advisor will be able to learn a lot about you quickly from the income statement and balance sheet and probably make some initial indications on how they can help you. Let's take them one at a time:

UNDERSTANDING WHAT YOU NEED

Income Statement

Add up your sources of income:

- Wages
- Rental Property
- Social Security or Other Benefits
- Pensions
- Investment Income
- Annuity Payments

Add up all of your expenses:

- Mortgage and/or Rent Payment
- Home Equity Payment
- Taxes
- Utilities
- Transportation (gas, repairs)
- Car Loan
- Credit Card Payments
- Student Loan Payments
- Groceries
- Clothing
- Entertainment and Dining Out
- Memberships
- Vacations
- Retirement and Investment Contributions

Now subtract the total of what you *spend* from your total *income* to get your *cash flow*. Is this number positive or negative?

If it is a negative it is likely that you are living beyond your means and on borrowed funds. You are likely to need someone who can help you manage credit and put you on the right road to a balanced budget.

Once your budget is balanced, then you can focus on investing toward future goals.

It is a great sign if your cash flow is positive. This indicates you are living within your means and should have additional dollars to put to work toward meeting your financial objectives. Thus, you should be working with an advisor who has experience in planning for the particular goals in which you have an interest, such as college funding or retirement planning, and who can also educate you about and guide you to appropriate investment vehicles and assets to help you work your way toward your goals. She should also assist you in defining actual dollar amounts to strive for in order to meet your objectives and help you determine what amount you should be putting away on a regular basis.

If your cash flow is negative but positive after removing "Retirement and Investment Contributions," then you do need to place some focus on budgeting, but you are in a good position to start saving toward your financial objectives more effectively.

Tax sensitivity is important when it comes to goal planning. Sometimes increasing positive cash flow can be achieved simply by changing how you are investing. If the types of investments you own are creating a lot of taxable income, your overall rate of return will be diminished. After all, it's not what you make, but what you keep! Proper utilization of retirement plans, tax deferred, and tax free vehicles are ways an advisor can help you become more tax efficient in your planning approach. The resulting decrease in income tax liability should have a positive impact on your cash flow.

Tax planning and finding an advisor who specializes in this area should be a priority in the event your taxes are a large percentage of your income. Though many advisors have basic tax knowledge and enough to assist those wishing to do tax efficient investing and goal funding, the more complex your situation, the greater importance needs to be placed on finding someone with expertise. This person might also be a tax preparer and/or an accountant.

For a lot of people, creating a balance sheet is easier than the income statement.

Balance Sheet

Add up everything you own:

- House Value
- Other Property (vacation home, real assets of significant value)
- Retirement Accounts
- Investment Accounts
- Savings Accounts
- Checking Accounts

Add up everything you owe:

- Mortgage
- Home Equity
- Car Loans
- Credit Cards
- Student Loans
- Personal Loans

Now subtract the total of what you *owe* from the total of what you *own*, and you will have your *net worth*. Is it positive or negative?

If it is negative, you are probably living beyond your means and relying on credit to get by. Budgeting will need to be addressed as part of your overall financial plan and before you tackle other financial goals and objectives.

Budgeting will also need to be addressed if your net worth is zero. In this case, you are essentially running in quicksand and getting nowhere, but you are at least in a position to make some adjustments so that you can start saving toward your financial goals, thus improving your net worth calculation as a result.

A positive net worth means that you are likely living within your means, probably have positive cash flow, and are already moving toward creating assets to fund financial objectives, even if it is unconsciously. You are in a good position to start fine-tuning your existing financial organization into a more efficient and effective financial plan. Many people in this position don't bother taking additional steps to define goals and put plans in place because there are no apparent problems. As one of my former associates used to say, "If you don't know where you're going, any road will take you there." You want to know where your destination is and determine the most efficient path to get you there. There are likely to be disruptions along the way. If you don't make provisions for these risks to your plan, they could become sinkholes that jeopardize your financial success. Just because there are no gaping problems, you can't become complacent. Don't be like so many Americans who spend more time planning their vacations than their financial futures!

QUICK TIPS

- Prepare a basic income statement and balance sheet to help you understand what you need from a financial advisor as well as get you organized to work with a professional.
- Understand how life events can affect your financial plans and when advice is needed and of what type.

Chapter 11

Choosing Advisors to Consider

Now that you've gotten to know your financial self a little better, it's time to go in search of your financial complement. This advisor or team of advisors will fill in the gaps between your own financial knowledge and what needs to be done to help you attain your financial and personal goals. Because you've taken the time to understand a little about your needs, you have a better idea of what type of financial professionals your situation requires.

Be sure to take this process seriously. You are not hiring someone to pave your driveway or plan a party. You are trying to find the right person to guide you toward financial success. Your goal is to find the right person with whom you can work for a long time, if not a lifetime. Changing financial advisors can cost you, so choose wisely the first time and perhaps you'll never have to make a change.

One of the best places to start is with your existing advisors. Speak with your accountant and lawyer about financial advisors they know. In the event you don't already utilize these types of services, ask other professionals with whom you come in contact such as your real estate agent or mortgage broker. More than likely they will have people to whom they can refer you, though be sure to gather as much information about these financial professionals as you can to be sure they are the type of advisors who can help you effectively. You should also find out if the referring party will be compensated in any way for providing a referral.

The benefit of obtaining names from your attorney or tax preparer or other type of professional with whom you've worked is that more than likely, they already have a pretty good idea of what your financial picture looks like and can hopefully point you in an applicable direction for financial help. Be sure to describe to them the type of help for which you are looking so they can be more thoughtful in any recommendations they give you. For example, you might say, "Larry, as you know we just had our first child, and we're really looking to make sure we do a good job preparing to pay for college." Or, "Linda, I am hoping to retire in five years, but am not sure if I've saved enough money and want to know how much more I need to put away." Qualifying statements like these will help your existing advisor pinpoint those financial professionals he or she knows who might be in the best position to help you.

The other benefit of asking an existing advisor about financial professionals with whom they have some experience is the idea behind team building. You want your tax preparer, attorney, financial advisor, and any other professional such as a mortgage professional to work together on your behalf. Introductions through existing relationships can create an integrated working team for you faster than building your network one advisor at a time.

Another way to gather candidate names is through friends, family members, and colleagues. Think about those individuals in your personal network who are most like you and have similar situations and challenges. Ask these people for names of their advisors, but also be sure that they are satisfied. Find out whether or not the advisors have particular areas of expertise and whether or not that knowledge matches up with your needs. You should also see if you can find out how the advisor gets paid and get a feel as to whether or not your connection views the relationship to be equitable. Ask how long the individual has engaged the advisor's services and whether or not there have ever been any problems. Ask about communication and accessibility. Does the advisor communicate regularly and proactively? Does your friend or family member feel comfortable contacting the advisor with questions or to provide updated information? How promptly does the advisor handle service requests (administrative changes or distribution of funds)?

There are also various organizations that can provide the names of advisors in your area as well as information about the individuals and their businesses:

Financial Planning Association

(800) 322-4237

www.fpaforfinancialplanning.org

National Association of Personal Financial Advisors

(847) 483-5400

www.napfa.org

Certified Financial Planner Board of Standards, Inc.

(800) 487-1497

www.cfp.net

QUICK TIPS

- Gather names of potential advisors from various sources.
- Compile as much information about advisor candidates from their referring sources as well as any available literature or online information.

Chapter 12

Choosing Candidates to Interview

Now that you have gathered the names of advisors to consider, what's next? You might want to narrow down the list to one that is manageable for the interview process. Keep in mind that each interview is likely to take 30 minutes or more plus travel time. You don't want to wear yourself out before the financial planning process has begun, so see if you can whittle your candidate list down to three names.

You can start by checking out the individuals and/or their organizations via FINRA or the SEC:

Financial Industry Regulatory Authority (FINRA)

(800) 289-9999

www.finra.org

Securities and Exchange Commission (SEC)

(800) SEC-0330

www.sec.gov

Internet searches can also be useful in learning about potential candidates. Keep in mind that what you find on the Internet might or might not be accurate; thus, you should be careful about how much you weigh Internet search data.

You might find websites for potential advisors that provide useful information. You could also request literature and brochures from the candidates' offices. In the event the advisor you are looking to hire is to provide investment advisory services, you should request a copy of the applicable ADV or "disclosure document."

You could learn a lot about your candidates through the process of requesting information. What did they provide and how quickly and thoroughly? Were they or their personnel pushy or stoic, or did they make you feel uncomfortable during any interactions that took place? Personality is important. An effective advisor-client relationship is one in which both parties can discuss finances and anything that affects them openly, including items that can be personal in nature such as health and relationships. Keep in mind the advisor must adhere to strict confidentiality policy. Your advisor will not be able to maximize his or her effectiveness if you feel uncomfortable discussing circumstances that affect your finances either directly or circuitously.

Hopefully, the information provided by the advisor and his or her staff will help you narrow down your choices. If not, you might want to consider criteria such as location: Is the advisor accessible from your home and/or office, and/or will he or she come to see you? What is his or her preferred method of communication (email, telephone, snail mail, face-to-face), and is it compatible with your own (and that of your spouse, if applicable)? Does he or she offer a complimentary initial meeting/interview? Do you meet his or her minimum investment requirements (some advisors have minimum account size requirements)?

Your goal should be to narrow down your list of potential advisors to three good candidates. After this is done, it is important to have an introductory meeting with each advisor. Many advisors will provide a complimentary initial meeting as an opportunity for you to get to know them and them to get to know you to see if a viable working relationship can be developed. This is certainly difficult to assess from just one meeting; thus, being prepared is key. The more prepared you are before your introductory sessions, the more you will get out of them.

QUICK TIPS

- Narrow down your list of advisor candidates to approximately three. Do this by reviewing information provided by the candidates, anything obtained through FINRA and the SEC or online, and by reviewing your own criteria.
- Start preparations for interviewing potential advisors.

Chapter 13

Interviewing Candidates

Because the process of choosing a financial advisor can be a bit daunting and intimidating, it is important to keep it moving along. Otherwise, you'll never get to the tasks at hand: financial goal setting, plan development, and implementation. It is for this reason interview appointments should be set in a timely manner, even on the same day if possible. If the process becomes drawn out, it might be more difficult to compare and contrast various advisors and what they can do for you.

Preparing for the Meeting

First find out how long you will have to meet with the advisor and what you should bring. Many advisors will have their own questionnaire to complete, though it can be time-consuming to complete these forms especially if you are interviewing multiple advisors. Keep in mind that the more prepared you are going into the meeting, the more you will get out of it. This does not mean you have to necessarily bear your financial soul, but the more you show the advisor, the more he is going to be able to show you what he can do for you.

Because you already put together an income statement (income resources minus outflows) and a balance sheet (what you own minus what you owe) back in Chapter 11, "Choosing Advisors to Consider," you're way ahead of the game! These documents are extremely helpful during an initial meeting; however, this information should be presented without account and Social Security numbers. Yes, I suffer from a touch of identity theft paranoia! But as my mother always says, "An ounce of prevention is worth a pound of cure." Though the investment industry is extremely sensitive to confidentiality issues, you just never know when someone might act negligently in regard to your own personal information. So until you've made a decision about hiring an advisor, there's no need to disclose such personal information.

In addition to the following, you might also consider bringing along your latest tax return for reference purposes. Along with the income statement (see Table 13.3) and the balance sheet (see Table 13.4), you should prepare the following lists:

- **Date(s) reports were prepared:**   Indicates whether or not the data the potential advisor is reviewing is current.
- **Family members with ages:**   Helps the potential advisor obtain an immediate understanding of your family structure and what financial obligations and objectives might already exist (see Table 13.1).[1]

Table 13.1   *Family Structure*

Name	Age
Sarah	52
Steven	51
Children:	
Scott	17
Susana	15

- **Prioritized financial goals:**   Lets the potential advisor know what your planning goals are and how they rank in importance (see Table 13.2).

---

[1]Tables 13.1–13.5 are for illustrative purposes only and do not reflect actual clients, portfolios, or recommendations.

Table 13.2 *Financial Goals*

College expense payments for two children

Retirement for Sarah and Steven when Sarah reaches age 65

Table 13.3 *Income Statement and Cash Flow*

Annual Income Resources

Sarah's gross salary (Project Manager)	$82,000
Steven's gross salary (Dental Hygienist)	$67,000
Total Gross Income:	**$149,000**

Annual Expenses

Mortgage Payment	$20,000
Home Equity Payment	$4,000
Income Taxes (federal and state)	$29,000
Property Taxes	$4,000
401(k) Investment	$30,000
Health Insurance	$4,000
Life Insurance	$1,000
Auto Insurance	$3,000
Property Insurance	$1,000
Phone/Internet/Cable	$1,500
Cell Phones	$1,500
Heat	$3,000
Electricity	$2,000
Groceries	$12,000
Transportation (gas and repairs)	$2,000
Car Loans	$2,000
Dental	$2,000

Table 13.3   *Income Statement and Cash Flow*

Annual Income Resources	
Pet Expenses	$1,500
Clothing/Equipment	$6,000
Dining Out	$2,000
Entertainment	$3,000
Vacations	$5,000
Memberships/Subscriptions	$1,000
Credit Card Repayment	$2,000
Miscellaneous	$1,500
Charitable Contributions	$3,000
Total Expenses:	**$147,000**

$149,000 − $147,000 = (Resources − Expenses)	$2,000 positive cash flow on an annual basis

Table 13.4   *Balance Sheet*

Sarah and Steven Own	Value
Home	$350,000
Sarah's 401(k)	$200,000
Steven's 401(k)	$350,000
Joint Savings	$15,000
Sarah's Checking	$3,000
Steven's Checking	$2,000
Scott's College Account	$25,000
Susana's College Account	$20,000
Total Equity:	**$965,000**

Table 13.4   *Balance Sheet*

Sarah and Steven Owe	Amount
Mortgage	$180,000
Home Equity	$20,000
Car Loan	$8,000
Credit Cards	$2,000
Total Amount Owed:	$210,000

Sarah and Steven's Net Worth	Net Worth
$965,000 - $210,000 =	$755,000
(Amount Owned - Amount Owed)	

- **Investment asset detail (statement copies can be used, but black out account and Social Security numbers):** Shows the potential advisor the types of investments with which you already have some experience. It also outlines who owns what in your family unit. This gives your candidate the opportunity to ask you questions in regard to how you feel about those investments and potentially obtain some gauge of your risk tolerance as well as your preferences regarding various types of investments and cost structures (see Table 13.5).

- **Potential financial fluctuations (inheritance, debts, projects, family status, or employment changes):** Allows the advisor the opportunity to anticipate change and provide you with some ideas on how they could affect you and what might be done to incorporate them efficiently into your plan.

For example:

Expenses can be rounded and estimated as long as cash flow is not a problem. If cash flow improvement is part of the overall financial goals, expense numbers should be accurate and specific. In this case, not much is left over; thus, Sarah and Steven may want to consider how they might adjust some of their expenses to help fund their other objectives.

The more clearly you are able to express your financial picture, the more efficient and effective your initial meeting will be. You will get more out of the meeting and could even determine you don't need an advisor or the particular advisor who you are interviewing. The advisor will be in a better position to provide information on how she will work with you and the costs associated with any recommended services. What's more, in the event you end up working with an advisor who charges by the hour, the more organized you are, the more money you will save if your information is provided to him in a well-prepared and easy to work with format as he shouldn't have to spend much, if any, of his own time, for which he is charging you his hourly rate, sorting through statements and arranging your data. Bringing electronically stored information on an excel spreadsheet can also make the financial planning process more efficient if the advisor has the means to work with your data without having to do much, if any, data entry.

These recommended documents are an important means to understanding how well you and the advisor candidate communicate. Preparation of these documents along with asking the right questions will not only provide you with answers, but will also help you gauge how well the advisor is actually listening to you. Communication is a two-way street in this situation and a key component in your relationship with your financial advisor. If you feel at all uncomfortable about discussing your financial and personal situations, goals, and objectives with the person you are interviewing, it could be time to move on to the next candidate. I've often heard about individuals feeling intimidated about their own lack of knowledge within a client-advisor relationship.

Tables 13.5 *Investment Asset Detail*

Susan's 401(k)	
ABC Company Stock	$30,000
Large Cap Growth Mutual Fund	$20,000
S&P 500 Index Fund	$30,000
Equity Income Mutual Fund	$30,000
International Mutual Fund	$20,000
Small Cap Mutual Fund	$20,000
Stable Value Fund	$50,000
Total:	**$200,000**
Steven's 401(k)	
Large Cap Growth Mutual Fund	$60,000
S&P 500 Index Fund	$60,000
Equity Income Mutual Fund	$60,000
International Mutual Fund	$30,000
Small Cap Mutual Fund	$40,000
Corporate Bond Fund	$50,000
High Yield Bond Fund	$50,000
Total:	**$350,000**
Scott's College Account	
Growth Mutual Fund	$5,000
Value Mutual Fund	$5,000
Corporate Bond Fund	$5,000
Fixed Account	$10,000
Total:	**$25,000**
Susana's College Account	
Growth Mutual Fund	$5,000
Value Mutual Fund	$5,000
Corporate Bond Fund	$5,000
Fixed Account	$5,000
Total:	**$20,000**

Keep in mind that this is why you are hiring an "expert." By going through this process, you have already come to terms with the idea that you can't or don't want to manage all or some of your finances alone. It is for this reason that you should never feel the least uncomfortable asking any questions or expressing your own interests or desires. This relationship is about you, your wants and desires, whether it is to get out of debt or to retire early.

During the Meeting

More than likely, the advisor will start out by giving you information about herself and the practice she runs. It is possible she will give you brochures: There will be time to look at those after you leave. Especially if you only have a short amount of time, set aside anything you can take with you to examine later. Take notes about the answers to the questions you ask, and be sure to observe nonverbal communication cues in addition to listening to what the candidate has to say. Pay careful attention to what the advisor has to say about your situation in order to evaluate how attentive the advisor is and how well she is listening. You might also observe whether or not the candidate is more interested in telling you all about herself, rather than finding out about you. There is a fine line between highly motivated financial advisors and those who may seem overly eager. It's a Goldilocks game: You want things to be "just right."

Keep in mind that Bernard Madoff's modus operandi was to make people feel as though he was doing them a tremendous favor. I suppose a client in such a position would be unlikely to rock the boat in any way, shape, or form and risk falling out of favor by asking too many questions. As you are interviewing candidates you want to keep this in mind. Do you really want to work with someone who seems unapproachable or to whom you must ingratiate yourself? You are likely to end up with a dysfunctional relationship that will be detrimental to your own financial planning in the long run. Keep in mind that you should be in the driver's seat in this situation; after all, it is your money, and you will be paying someone to perform services for you, much like you would a dentist or a contractor for your home. If you cannot effectively express your goals and desires or ask questions because you are afraid of taking the advisor's time or that you will be unfavorably judged, then this is not the most productive relationship for you. You must remember that you are hiring him, not the other way around.

On the flip side, if an advisor is too eager to please, this can also be a red flag for a potential dysfunctional relationship. Victims of my ex-husband, who were also friends of ours, once told me he was really pushing to get them to invest more money with him toward "the end." I imagine he would have said and done most anything the more desperate he got to fund his floundering Ponzi scheme. While this is an extreme case, there may be other reasons why an advisor might be overly interested in working with you that might be in conflict with what is in your best interest. For example, the advisor may have

- Hefty corporate and/or personal expenses and needs your business to help keep him afloat.

- A significant ego to feed and more interested in growing his own business and/or wallet than serving your needs. I once met an advisor who considered himself the "McDonald's of Financial Planning." This indicated to me that this individual was interested in high volume and not necessarily the individuals he might be serving.

- Unrealistic expectations about how much he can actually do for each individual client.

- Little experience in the field and might just be starting to build his own business.

While enthusiasm and aggressiveness can be good qualities in a financial advisor, if they are not directed as a means to service you and your best interests, they can work against you and your financial goals.

There is a wide spectrum of advisors out there. You are charged with finding the one, or combination of individuals, who has the knowledge, ability, and desire to help you achieve your financial goals. As you might have noticed, this process can be a bit consuming, but the investment in time is worth it. The financial advisor–client relationship should be one that is long-term, if not lifelong. Changing advisors can be expensive and detrimental to making progress toward financial goals. Thus, you want to make the right decision initially, and hopefully that will be the last time you'll ever have to go through this process!

So what are the right questions to ask in order to gather enough information to aid you in your decision? The first question to ask is about time: "How much time will we have today?" This way you can gauge how quickly you should keep things moving along, while providing you with clues on how packed the advisor keeps her schedule. If you only have a short amount of time, be sure to prioritize these questions so that you get the most important ones answered. Some advisors will only provide 15 minutes for a "getting to know you" visit. While this could seem stingy, it could also indicate that they are more dedicated to their existing clientele than adding new ones, which is not necessarily a bad thing.

- How long have you been in business?
- What credentials and licenses do you have?
- What is your educational background?
- In what area(s) do you specialize?
- Tell me about your typical client.
- What would your clients say about you?

- What services do you provide, and what are the associated costs?
- How do you get paid for your services?
- What is the level of assets you have under management?
- How many clients do you have?
- What is your typical account size?
- How are assets managed, and what resources are employed?
- Do you utilize other investment managers? If so, who are they, and are there any referral fee arrangements involved?
- What is the structure of your office and staff?
- Will I be interacting with you or a staff member?
- How do you communicate with clients and how often?
- How often do you meet with clients?
- What is your investment philosophy?
- How often are portfolios rebalanced?
- What do you expect from your clients?
- Would you ever consider "firing" a client? If so, under what circumstances?
- Have you had any formal client complaints?
- Who is your broker/dealer, and how do they support your business?
- Who is the asset custodian, how much insurance (SIPC and other) coverage do account holders have, and how does the coverage protect assets?
- What do you like most about the business you're in?
- What do you like least about your business?

In the event the advisor's firm acts as it's own asset custodian, as was the case with Bernard Madoff, you will want to ask about the firm's auditor and ask the following questions:

- Who is the auditor, and what is their relationship with the firm?
- How frequently are audits performed?
- Are audits planned or spontaneous?
- What internal controls does the firm employ to prevent theft?

You also might want to ask the advisor about his own succession plans. In other words, what happens to clients if something happens to the advisor? After you've been so diligent in choosing someone, it would be nice to know that you won't have to go through it again if the advisor becomes ill, disabled, or worse, or chooses to retire from the business.

You should ask the advisor his opinion about your situation as you've laid it out. Find out what services the candidate recommends for you and about approximate costs and time frames that might be involved. The advisor is not likely to give you specific recommendations at this time but should be able to give you an idea of what he can do for you.

Finally, be sure to ask the advisor candidates for references. Though they are likely to provide you with contacts who are satisfied clients, it doesn't hurt to speak with others who have working experience with the advisor. You should ask the advisor to provide you with names of people with similar goals and who are in comparable life situations. Though you are unlikely to learn about the specifics of a client, you should be able to get a feel for the advisor's demeanor, communication and investment styles, thoroughness, and approachability.

After the Meeting

Immediately after the meeting, you should jot down any additional notes you did not have an opportunity to take during the meeting and perhaps give the advisor a rating on various levels such as

- Did the advisor answer your questions thoroughly?
- Was the advisor attentive and focused?
- Did the advisor's plans for you seem realistic?
- Does the advisor's experience and education complement your needs?
- What is your interpretation of the advisor's fee structure, and is it appropriate for your situation?
- Did the advisor follow up with you after the meeting with a thank you, summary, and/or answers and information that was not furnished during the meeting?
- What is your comfort level in communicating with the advisor?

Though you should prioritize your criteria for hiring an advisor, don't forget that you are buying the whole package. If you are only focused on fees and/or costs, you can miss out on advice quality or settle for inefficient communication. Keep in mind that many times you do get what you pay for! On the flip side, if you are only concerned with the quality of the communication, you could be sacrificing advice capacity or end up paying through the nose for a warm and fuzzy relationship.

Be sure to call the references. Most likely they are expecting to hear from you, so the conversation shouldn't be awkward. Questions to consider asking include

- How long have you worked with the advisor?
- What services has the advisor provided?

- How do you communicate with the advisor and how often?
- How often are changes made in your portfolio and for what reasons?
- How ethical do you think the advisor is?
- Have you ever had an issue with the advisor? If so, how quickly and thoroughly was it resolved?
- Have you ever considered changing advisors? If so, why?
- Has the advisor performed relatively well in both good and bad markets?
- Would you recommend this advisor to your child/parent/sibling/best friend?
- Do you know anyone else who is working with the advisor you might call?

At this point, you should review any materials you have collected. If the advisor is a Registered Investment Advisor (RIA) or Investment Advisor Representative (IAR), these materials will include the Form ADV. According to the Securities and Exchange Commission's website, "Form ADV has two parts. Part 1 contains information about the adviser's education, business, and disciplinary history within the last ten years and is filed electronically with the SEC. Part 2 includes information on an adviser's services, fees, and investment strategies. Currently, the SEC does not require advisers to file Part 2 electronically." However, your advisor is required to furnish you with Part 2 prior to entering into an investment advisory agreement if he is providing investment advice. More information about the Form ADV can be found on the SEC's website at www.sec.org.

If you have discovered other entities with which you could be potentially involved, be sure to check them out as well. See what information is available about the broker/dealers the potential advisors are utilizing on the SEC and FINRA websites as well as the sites of the entities themselves. Also check on the potential custodians to be sure your assets are going to a valid entity that will provide you with protection against firm failure. Thus, they should provide Securities Investor Protection Corporation coverage and likely some private insurance as well. You can check on the SIPC website at www.sipc.org to verify the custodians or broker-dealers are part of the SIPC member database.

If you have any lingering questions for any of your candidates at this point, call or email them promptly. You've come this far, and you don't want to hold up the decision-making process too much longer. There is a fine line between doing your own due diligence and over-analyzing. As one of my former colleagues, James Keefe, CFA, used to say, "Over-analysis leads to paralysis."

Once you have collected all the pertinent information, reviewed it, and applied it to your prioritized criteria, it is time to make a decision. The answer could be obvious or not. In the event the decision making is close, you might just have to go with your gut instinct.

QUICK TIPS

- Be as prepared as possible when meeting with an advisor for an evaluation interview.
- Pay attention to nonverbal as well as verbal communication.
- Evaluate how well the advisor communicates with you: how carefully he or she listens to you about your situation as well as your goals and objectives.
- Be sure to obtain answers to all of your questions during or after the meeting if necessary.
- Check advisor references.
- Check out the advisor's affiliates: broker/dealer and/or custodian as well as auditor if applicable.

Chapter 14

Spotting Red Flags: Advisors to Avoid

Unfortunately, taking a leap of faith is part of hiring a financial advisor. If you do your homework, most likely it will work out for the best. At the very least, you will keep your assets and peace of mind out of harm's way by avoiding the Bradford Bleidts and Bernard Madoffs of the financial advice world. Fortunately, there really are more decent financial advisors out there who are dedicated to the craft and their clients than there are evil ones who are only out for themselves.

Red flags can pop up at various stages during your journey in search of the perfect advisor. Pay attention to them as they will not only help you narrow down your list of potential candidates, but they might actually save you some or a lot of grief down the road.

The Name and Information Gathering Phase

As you collect names of potential advisors to interview, do a FINRA broker check on those who are "Registered Representatives" at www.finra.org/Investors/ToolsCalculators/BrokerCheck/index.htm. You can look up the advisor and his or her broker/dealer to see if there have been any customer disputes or regulatory and disciplinary events. The report also tells you in what states the advisor is licensed, what licensing exams he or she has passed, and about the advisor's employment history. Firm reports also provide information on regulatory and disciplinary events, as well as a profile, history, and information on operations. Keep in mind that most firms have hundreds, if not thousands of advisors associated with them. Thus, any arbitration, regulatory, or disciplinary problems might not necessarily reflect the particular advisor with whom you are considering doing business. Most reputable firms who have had issues typically take steps via their compliance department to see that future problems are avoided as it is in their best interest to avoid arbitration, regulatory, and disciplinary problems. Not that you should ignore negative event history. It is worthwhile asking questions about pertinent matters and what the firm has done to prevent future problems.

If the advisor with whom you are doing business is a Registered Investment Advisor (RIA) or Investment Advisor Representative (IAR) associated with an RIA, you can search for the advisor's or firm's Form ADV via the Securities and Exchange Commission's website at www.adviserinfo.sec.gov/IAPD/Content/Search/iapd_OrgSearch. aspx. This application for registration contains a wealth of information covering business activities, affiliations, custodial arrangements, state registrations, employees, clients, compensation, as well as any disciplinary history.

Should you discover any grave discrepancies through this discovery phase or feel uneasy about any reported arbitration, regulatory, or disciplinary events, you should take this as an opportunity to ask questions, which you may want to save for a face-to-face meeting to see how the advisor reacts, or take it as a "red flag" and move on to the next name on your list. Should you chose to ask more questions, be sure that the explanation you receive is satisfactory before dismissing the discovery as a minimal factor in your decision-making process.

If the advisor's firm acts as its own custodian, as Bernard Madoff's firm supposedly did, it is time to check out the firm's auditor. You might want to request a copy of the firm's most recent audit and its findings. If you find a lack of cooperation with this verification process or you find information about the auditor difficult to obtain, this could be a red flag. You might want to check out the American Institute of Certified Public Accountants website at www.aicpa.org for more information on the firm.

If the advisor is a CERTIFIED FINANCIAL PLANNER™ professional, you can see if there has been any applicable disciplinary history through the Certified Financial Planner Board of Standards, Inc. along with checking out their certification status via www.cfp.net/search/. Again, any grave discrepancies or troubling history should send that red flag waving. For example, if you look up my ex-husband, Bradford Bleidt, you will see that his certification has been revoked along with a description of his violations of the CFP Board's Code of Ethics and Professional Conduct.

For Certified Public Accountants, disciplinary history can be searched on the American Institute for Certified Public Accountants website at www.aicpa.org/pubs/cpaltr/disciplinary_actions/sortlist.aspx.

If the potential advisor has already sent you a list of references, it might not hurt to call them before you have a meeting with the candidate as you might get a better feel for who he or she is. You might also obtain names from the references of others who are or have been clients of the advisor previously who might be able to give you some valuable information. In speaking with people who have employed the advisor, you should be looking for information in regard to whether the advisor

- Works with people who have similar circumstances to yours
- Has a communication style consistent with your expectations
- Disappointed any clients in any way and if so, how
- Performed relatively well in good and poor market periods
- Provided you with any information that is in conflict with what existing or former clients say about him or her

During the Meeting

Your challenge while interviewing a financial advisor candidate is to employ your powers of observation as well as you can to

- Detect important inconsistencies with any information conveyed to you verbally by the advisor, advisor's staff, clients, or former clients or provided in any literature. Major inconsistencies could be clues about whether or not the advisor is too busy to keep his or her facts straight or an indication that the advisor may say anything to get your business.

- Determine how well you communicate with the advisor about important matters. If you have any difficulty following anything the advisor discusses with you, be sure to ask for clarification. After all, this is all about you and your money, and you should be able to effectively and efficiently exchange information with your advisor.

- Perceive whether your business is not particularly important to the advisor or potentially vital. Either could be a red flag for service quality or worse, considering Bernard Madoff had a way of making those who did business with him feel fortunate for having the privilege of doing so. Bradford Bleidt was desperate to get new money in the door any way he could and may have appeared overly eager to please, especially in the end.

- Evaluate the advisor's organization and preparedness for the meeting, especially if you sent information about you and your situation ahead of time.

- Identify whether or not the advisor acknowledges how important this initial introductory meeting is for you. If the candidate is constantly taking telephone calls or being interrupted with other matters during time that should be set aside for you, it could be an indication that the advisor is incapable of making time for you once you are a paying customer.

- Clarify custodial arrangements for any assets that will be invested. Any ambiguity surrounding this issue should be considered a red flag. No transfers should be made or checks written until you are absolutely confident about what institution will be holding your funds. No checks representing investable assets should be written to the advisor personally. In most cases, checks will be written to a custodian or wirehouse (such as Merrill Lynch or Morgan Stanley Smith Barney) providing SIPC Inc. (the Securities Investor Protection Corporation) coverage and possibly additional insurance protection. If the investment advisor's firm performs custodial functions via the use of an omnibus account, be sure to find out who the firm's auditor is and what practices are employed to protect client funds.

- Understand potential compensation arrangements and how much engaging the advisor may end up costing you. The advisor should be able to give you an idea of how they will charge you: assets under management, commissions, fees, or a combination of structures, and provide you with an idea of what costs might be involved. Ambiguity about how the advisor is compensated can also be a red flag, as in the extreme case with Bernard Madoff who didn't seem to charge fees. Keep in mind that a good advisor should be compensated reasonably, and you, as the client, should have a good understanding how that compensation is derived.

- Solicit recommendations. Though the advisor is unlikely to develop a specific strategy for you on the spot especially without an executed agreement, you should be able to get an idea of what the candidate is thinking will work best for you along with a description of what steps it will take to start moving in the right direction.

- Ask for referrals. If the advisor is unwilling or unable to provide you with contact information of existing clients, consider it a concern. Though there are confidentiality issues when it comes to the world of personal finance, most good advisors have clients who are willing to speak to potential new clients on their behalf in these situations.

After the Meeting

After you have met with the advisor it is a good idea to take some notes about your perceptions during the meeting especially if you are meeting with a number of candidates. Be sure to detail anything that might have occurred during the meeting that caused you to be uncomfortable in any way especially anything that could impede a functional relationship with the advisor.

It is important to follow up with any referral contacts given to you in the meeting. Though it might seem to be a useless exercise given that you are most likely to receive a list of clients acting as cheerleaders for the advisor candidate, you never know what you could learn. Should you hear anything negative through your conversations, this could be very telling given that a client serving as a referral is not expected to provide anything but positive feedback. At the very least you will get a feel for the types of people with whom the advisor works and whether or not they have similar financial circumstances to your own.

It is not uncommon for an advisor to follow up with you with some form of recap of the meeting. This can give you the opportunity to determine how well the advisor was listening to you and interpreting your financial situation and goals. There might also be matters that were left unsettled either because of additional data about you requested by the advisor or materials and information promised to you. In the event the advisor candidate is not responsive in providing agreed upon follow-up items, consider this as a potential organizational or interest level problem on the part of the professional. In other words, the professional was not organized enough to get what was promised to you, or it was not a priority to do so. Either is a concern.

Advisors to Avoid

Up to this point, if you've done the leg work and all of your homework, it is time to narrow the choices by removing candidates who could be problematic. This could include those who

- Have a disturbing disciplinary history with FINRA, the SEC, or any other professional organization to which they belong or once belonged.

- Cannot adequately show you where your assets will be held and in what ways they will or will not be protected. Keep in mind that SIPC and similar insurances do not protect your assets against market fluctuation. These coverages are available to protect customers from the failure of a covered brokerage firm. Thus, any advisor who "over promises" in regard to what these types of insurances offer investors is someone to steer clear of. They are either untrained or manipulative. Neither are qualities you want in a financial advisor.

- Are unable to communicate with you effectively. This is not necessarily an indication that a candidate is incompetent or dishonest. However, the relationship you have with your financial advisor is incredibly important. People have different communication styles, and sometimes they just don't mesh. You do not want to find yourself in this situation with your financial advisor. They can't help you if you don't feel comfortable opening up to them. They also can't help you if they are unable to communicate their ideas, advice, and recommendations to you in a way that you can absorb and implement them.

- Provide ambiguous explanations about potential investment strategies. The advisor should be able to give you reasonable guidance about the strategies he or she is intending to employ and be willing to educate you about them.

- Avoid providing you with a reasonable explanation about how they get paid and applicable costs affecting your situation. Again, you should understand the advisor's compensation structure and how it affects you and potentially your investments for the long term.

- Don't measure up in the eyes of their referrals especially if a lack of satisfaction is consistent over a number of contacts. If the advisor is unaware of problems existing with those clients he or she has chosen to endorse them, there probably is trouble in paradise.

- Furnish information verbally or through brochures or other sales materials that is inconsistent or in conflict with other available information, such as what is published on the websites of the SEC and FINRA. For example, is the advisor claiming that he is a CFP® practitioner when he has not yet, in fact, finished all of his requirements? If so, this is the type of grave inconsistency that should not be overlooked.

- Disclose any confidential information about existing or former clients without permission from them. Confidentiality is imperative to the advisor-client relationship, not to mention required by regulatory and professional organizations.

Identifying whether or not any of the red flag conditions exist can help you narrow down your list of potential candidates and hopefully keep you out of harm's way at the same time. Utilize the rest of the information you gathered throughout your fact finding mission to help you pinpoint the candidate who is going to be best for you. In the event that relationship does not work out for some reason, you've probably created a decent back-up list through the process, so hold on to those names in case you need them.

QUICK TIPS

- Be sure to ask an advisor about any negative regulatory or disciplinary events you uncover during your investigation as well as what steps the advisor and his or her firm have taken to prevent future problems.

- Be wary of any discrepancies you discover or a lack of a desire on the potential advisor's part to provide you with requested information.

- Evaluate whether or not you and the advisor can effectively communicate about important matters.

- Clearly understand the strategies that could be employed in your situation.

- Verify custodial arrangements for assets.

- Uncover potential compensation arrangements and determine whether or not they are in line with your expectations.

- Check references.

Chapter 15

The Rules of Engagement

The process of hiring a financial advisor has become more formalized as the industry has matured. In the past it would have been typical for an account to be opened and a discussion about goals to take place and possibly a financial plan prepared. Today it is more common to find additional documentation in the way of a financial planning and/or asset management agreement to be signed along with a risk management profile if you are entering into an investment advisory arrangement. While all these legal documents seem to make the process more cumbersome, and they do in certain situations help to protect the entity with which you are doing business, they are mainly there to protect you, the client. They are required by the SEC and the States for Registered Investment Advisors (RIAs) for managed assets. A typical Investment Management Agreement will address issues such as

- **Account Title:** How the account is to be owned; joint, individual, trust, retirement, and so on.

- **Service Expectations:** How assets will be managed, what types of securities will be used, and whether or not the advisor and/or firm will have discretionary authority over the account, which is the ability to execute asset trades in the account without client consultation and consent.

- **Custodial Arrangements:** What entity will hold the assets.

- **Transactions:** What entity will be responsible for transactions.

- **Reporting:** What types of reports will be provided and how frequently.

- **Fees:**   How asset management fees will be assessed and when as well as how assets under management will be determined for fee calculation purposes and then collected.

- **Investment Objective:**   How the firm defines various investment objectives such as aggressive growth, growth, growth with income, balanced, conservative growth, income, and so on.

- **Confidentiality:**   When it is acceptable for the firm to disclose information about client identity and/or financial affairs.

- **Client Responsibilities:**   What is expected of the client in regard to keeping the advisory firm up-to-date about changes in circumstances and investment objectives.

- **Risk:**   What risks are involved with investing in typical securities used by the advisor such as market, currency, economic, political, interest rate, reinvestment, liquidity, inflation, default, and business. This paragraph typically states that the client assumes the risks described and that not all investment decisions will be profitable. It also limits the liability of the advisor and firm as long as client instructions have been followed.

- **Notification:**   How the client should communicate with the firm in order to change instructions such as investment objective.

- **ADV Disclosure:**   Acknowledgement that the Form ADV Part II was received by the client.

- **Arbitration:**   A description of the dispute resolution process, to what claims it applies in regard to controversy over the client account.

- **Proxy Voting:**   What the firm's policy is on shareholder communications and voting in regard to securities held in the client's account.

- **Termination:** How the contract is terminated and remaining investment management fees are calculated, as well as the disclosure of whether or not termination fees will be imposed.

The contract is typically generic in nature and personalized for each client account. So if you have a joint account, two IRAs, and two Coverdell IRAs, which will be managed by the selected advisor, you will have to execute five sets of paperwork. Your advisor and/or his or her staff should be able to walk you through the agreement to be sure you understand each item in the event any explanation is needed before executing the document. The areas that are personalized for your particular account are Account Title, Fees, and Investment Objective. Be sure the account titling is accurate, the fees are what you agreed to, and the investment objective is correct. If the investment objective is not accurate, you could end up with investments in your portfolio that are not appropriate for you and might not have much recourse in the event that they don't serve you well. It is for this reason it is important that you understand what you are signing and that customized fields have been personalized in a way that is appropriate for you and your situation. Also be sure to verify who the stated custodian is as well as the broker/dealer. If you have not yet checked out these entities, it is time to do so before you sign on the dotted line or move any money.

A Financial Planning Agreement might contain much of the same information and acknowledgements as an Investment Management Agreement, though it will also provide descriptions of the various planning options offered by the firm such as

- **Investment Planning:** Determination of appropriate asset allocation and/or security selection given the client's goals, time horizon, risk tolerance, tax situation, existing assets, and income. Keep in mind that portfolio development is different from ongoing asset management; thus, it

113

falls under a "financial planning" agreement as opposed to the "investment management" agreement. The advisor might or might not be part of the implementation process. If the advisor is also assisting with implementation, it should be understood whether or not there are additional fees and/or commissions and whether or not a "fee off-set" situation exists. In other words, will any commissions earned offset the assessed fee? This should be disclosed in the agreement. Advisors, in some cases, may charge both portfolio development fees and ongoing asset management fees. Under these circumstances both a financial planning and an asset/investment management agreement should be executed.

- **Tax Planning:** Analysis of the existing tax situation, income tax liability reduction technique recommendations, and possibly preparation of tax documents.

- **Estate Planning:** Preparation for the preservation and efficient transfer of assets to the next generation and/or beneficial entities, including charitable. Plan development and execution will typically require the involvement of an attorney if the advisor is not a member of the legal profession, to prepare legal documents. Typical documents most people should execute and keep up-to-date include the will (directs how and to whom assets should be transferred), health care directives (appoints individuals to make health care decisions in the event of incapacitation), and power of attorney (appoints individuals to make business decisions in the event of incapacitation).

- **Cash Flow and Budgeting:** Analysis of existing sources of income and spending habits most needed in cases of negative cash flow, increasing debt balances, and declining or stagnant net worth growth. Planning recommendations might include debt restructuring to reduce interest rates and potentially payments, setting reasonable spending objectives as well as developing goals for saving.

- **Retirement:** Determination of the future cost of retirement based upon desired spending, understanding of existing and potential resources (pension, Social Security), development of a savings plan road map based on time frame, risk tolerance, and incorporation of other goals, such as college funding.

- **Risk Management (Insurance):** Analysis of existing vulnerabilities to personal liability and loss as well as existing assets and protective programs already in place to discover gaps where coverage is needed. Risk management planning also means understanding existing resources, what risks are affordable to self-insure. Resulting recommendations may be to alter or purchase additional automobile, homeowners, umbrella, health, disability, life and/or long-term care insurance coverage.

- **College Funding:** Determination of the future cost of higher learning institutions for each potential student involved as well as identification of existing resources and possible support programs. Recommendations might include savings amounts and vehicles for the particular purpose of education funding, such as utilization of the 529 Plan and the Coverdell Education Savings Account (ESA) or Education IRA to help with the tax efficient savings of education funds and/or shifting of assets for better aid qualification purposes.

- **Comprehensive Financial Planning:** Complete analysis of existing assets, debt and cash flow, titling of assets, existing investments, income tax situation, as well as estate and risk management structures. A comprehensive financial plan will assist with goal setting in each of these areas as well as retirement and college funding where appropriate and provide recommendations and action steps to be taken to obtain a well-rounded and realistic financial picture.

A financial planning agreement can be all inclusive or "a la carte." Make sure you understand what you are ordering and how it is priced to be sure you are not paying for services you don't need.

Whether you elect asset management services, comprehensive, or specific goal type planning or a combination, your goals, plan, and progress should be reviewed on a regular basis. If you elect asset management services, more than likely your advisor will be doing this with you minimally on an annual basis as part of a yearly review. After all you are paying fees on a regular basis. When you elect planning services, you pay to purchase a plan based on your circumstances at the time the plan was done. Thus, it could be up to you to request a review with your advisor. On a minimal basis, you should review your plan every five years and/or as a result of any major life change: marriage, divorce, child, death, illness, job change, or in the event of major market and/or economic changes for long-range planning. As your goal time frame changes, the review frequency schedule should be stepped up to an annual basis visitation. One thing to note, and it is a mistake I've seen frequently made by investors, is that as you get closer to a goal, your time frame shortens. The tendency is to want to put the "pedal to the metal" and become more aggressive, when actually the opposite is true. As you get closer to needing assets to pay for college or retirement or any other savings goal, becoming more conservative will help ensure your hard earned assets are there when it is time to pay the piper. Otherwise, it's just a gamble. Your financial advisor should help you with this adjustment as you get closer to your goals.

Once you have hired an advisor and executed the appropriate agreements you can start moving forward with planning. If you are, in fact, doing financial planning, the advisor might need to collect more specific data depending on what you provided during the initial interview. Depending on whether you are doing comprehensive or specific goal planning, the advisor will need to know and or collect some or all of the following:

- Specific demographics of the family unit, including those of parents living or deceased
- Derivation of family income (paycheck stubs)
- Current tax situation (income tax return)
- Details of current spending and how it may or may not change in retirement (budgets)
- Information on any retirement benefits including pensions, Social Security, employer contribution rates to 401(k), or other defined contribution plan (statements)
- Particulars of any life, disability, long-term care, liability, and property insurances: risks covered, amounts, limitations, deductibles, duration, riders, premiums, group or individual (policies)
- Breakdown of investments: cost basis, where held, how titled, number of shares, use of assets, dividends, and capital gains (statements)
- Expectations of children attending college: how many years, public or private school
- Essentials of any estate planning (documents)
- Potential of any large expenditures, windfalls, or changes affecting the existing financial structure

Once the advisor has gathered all of the pertinent information, it is his or her job to analyze the existing situation, convert the funding goals into real numbers, and work with you to come up with a feasible plan to implement either with or without the advisor's help. In most cases and depending on when financial planning starts, additional funds are needed in order to successfully travel the road to big goal financing. The financial advisor can hopefully work with you to locate additional funds or determine how they will be added over time now that he or she has a good handle on your whole financial picture.

For example, if we look at Sarah and Steven again, they have a large funding goal that most of us share: to retire one day. They would like to retire in 13 years and maintain a similar standard of living. They don't expect to make too many changes in their lifestyle, though they would like to travel a bit more. They expect their children to be self-sufficient by then. Their current spending is $147,000 per year. Some expenses will go down or be eliminated:

- Saving for college
- Saving for retirement
- Mortgage and home equity payments (unless home equity is tapped to pay for college)
- Auto loans
- Income taxes
- Utilities and cell phones
- Auto expenses
- Groceries
- Clothing

Some expenses will go up significantly:

- Medical
- Dental
- Vacation

And most likely everything will go up, except their pensions, due to inflation.

Sarah and Steven currently have $550,000 saved for retirement. They expect that amount to grow at a rate of 8% on average per year, and they expect to continue to contribute $30,000 per year to their retirement plans. Should they follow this disciplined course, they will have over two million dollars when they retire. Though this sounds like a nice chunk of change, if we factor in inflation at the rate of 4%, it is worth just over a million in today's dollars.

Sarah and Steven believe they can live on approximately $50,000 per year in retirement, which is approximately 90% of their current living expenses without the mortgages, savings, and income tax payments. Of course, income taxes don't go away in retirement, but they can be reduced if the gross income number is lower, which it will be in this case. So Sarah and Steven believe they will need approximately $67,000 before taxes. Well, that's today's dollars. What about in 13 years? Again using a 4% inflation rate, they will need approximately $113,000 before taxes per year to continue their lifestyle as is. So the big question is, will they have enough, or should they be saving more? It's better to find out now than when you arrive at retirement's doorstep. If they need $113,000 per year and their asset base is $2,230,000 they would be withdrawing approximately 5% per year. Five percent is not necessarily a conservative number. I would be more comfortable with a withdrawal rate of 4%, which gives them $89,000 which is almost $24,000 short of their goal.

So what are their choices?

- Gamble and hope for the best.
- Live on $2,000 less per month in retirement.
- Save an additional $2,000 per month now so they have closer to $2,800,000 in retirement (their current cash flow only provides for $167 dollars of additional savings each month).
- Look at other resources such as pensions, Social Security, earned income.

In this case, let's assume Sarah will have a pension that should cover the shortfall, which is great news given they don't want to have to depend on Social Security.

But, of course, with the best-laid plans come bumps in the road. While Steven and Sarah are doing a great job saving for retirement, they are not financially prepared to send their kids to college. Thus, they are not likely to have as many resources in retirement as hoped unless their children receive aid, their children pay for their own school, the whole family cuts back on spending so more can be saved, or a combination of these alternatives. Other issues that can throw a wrench into their retirement plan are

- Death or disability of Sarah or Steven
- Illness within the family
- Divorce
- Other financial calamity such as a lawsuit

It is for these reasons risk management aspects (insurances) should be reviewed in conjunction with planning. It is also why the entire plan should be reviewed periodically especially as Sarah and Steven get closer to retirement.

If you are hiring an advisor to manage your investments only, goal setting and planning are still extremely important, though they might not be as intricate and involved as doing comprehensive or goal-specific financial planning. Regardless, an asset manager needs direction, too. If your advisor has a good understanding of what your goals are, how many years you have to collect and grow assets, what your existing asset base is and how it is invested, and how your investments might be affected by taxes, he will be in a better position to effectively invest whatever you are turning over to him as well as manage your own expectations. You might think that your investment objective is growth, but when your advisor sees that you only have five years to save for your goal, he will likely feel differently. After all, five years is not a very long time in investment terms. It is for this reason a risk profile is used before any investing takes place. The profile is a tool used by the advisor in selecting an appropriate asset allocation and specific investments based on your time horizon, tax situation, and comfort level. It is also a document that can help you, the customer, in the event the advisor chooses investments for you that are not in line with the results of the risk profile. It will ask you questions that will help the advisor identify how long until you may need to tap into investment resources, how long you have been investing, and with what types of products you have experience, and how you feel about market fluctuation.

Many profiles talk about investment risk tolerance in terms of percentage. In other words, they ask the questions, "At what level of portfolio loss would you begin to feel uncomfortable?"

0–5%

6–10%

11–15%

16–20%

More than 20%

While the question does inspire the investor to think in terms of volatility and loss, I find the use of percentages does not always hit home. As the investor, you should take these percentages and understand what they translate into in regard to real hard-earned dollars. So if you had a portfolio worth $100,000 and were asked the question, think of the answers in terms of what the percentages mean in actual dollar amounts lost:

$0–$5,000

$6,000–$10,000

$11,000–$15,000

$16,000–$20,000

More than $20,000

Thinking about what you could potentially lose in dollars instead of percentages might alter how you answer the question.

Also as we have learned over 2008 and into 2009, very "traditional" types of investments can lose much more than 20% during periods of crisis. For example, who would have ever thought that companies like General Motors, Bank of America, and Citigroup could have traded down over 90% of their value just a year or so earlier?

I have also found that people's risk tolerance changes. When the market goes up, I find people to be very risk tolerant and will communicate their lack of fear of market fluctuation: that they understand it happens and they're in it for the long term. It is very easy to be risk tolerant when investments are going up. When the market goes down drastically, many of these same individuals become doom and gloomers and lose that bravery they had when their investments were going up. You need to be honest with yourself in measuring risk tolerance in order to avoid future disappointments or fearful situations. The reason this is so important is because our emotions tell us to do the exact opposite of what we should be doing when it comes to investing. We are driven by fear and greed, which tell us to buy when assets are overpriced and sell when they are at bargain levels. Your advisor can help you deal with your emotions but only if you honestly communicated your true risk tolerance.

In the event you choose to hire multiple investment advisors, it could be important to keep each of them updated on what the others are doing. Though it is more traditional and certainly simpler to work with only one, some investors are choosing to hire multiple advisors in the wake of the Bernard Madoff scandal. It's along the lines of "not putting all of your eggs in one basket." Yet this is exactly what can happen if you keep your advisors in the dark about each other. They will be operating in an information void. If you keep your advisors up to date about your other investments, they can tailor what they are managing to complement what you have elsewhere.

Once your goals are set and the plans made, it is time to get the assets to work. This might mean investing a lump sum or moving assets around if you are having the chosen advisor implement recommended plans and/or manage the assets. Though there has been much talk about a "paperless society," unfortunately that is not the case in the investment world. As with the investment management agreement, you will have to sign an account form for each individual, retirement, trust, and/or education account to be opened. Retirement and trust accounts may have additional paperwork as well. Be prepared to provide

- Mailing address that is not a post office box
- Telephone number, date of birth, Social Security number
- Employment position, employer, address, and telephone number
- Annual income
- Net worth (what you own minus what you owe)
- Liquid assets (total of cash, money market and bank accounts, investment and retirement accounts)
- Tax bracket
- Investment objective
- Investment experience
- Risk tolerance
- Time horizon
- Marital and dependent status
- Affiliation with stock exchanges, banks, trust companies, and/or insurance companies
- Information as to whether or not you are a 10% or more shareholder of a publicly traded company, a policy-making executive, and/or an employee or related to an employee of such entities
- Desired treatment of sales proceeds (have them sent to you or held in cash)

- Direction for dividends, interest, and capital gains (whether you want them added to cash, sent to you, or reinvested)
- How you want asset purchases treated (held in account or certificate form)
- A government issued photo ID such as a driver's license or passport

All of this information is collected on your account agreement, which is a confidential document. You will need to complete one for each account you open. In the event you are opening a retirement or a "transfer on death" account, you will also need to identify your beneficiaries and provide address, date of birth, and Social Security information for them.

On top of all that, if you are transferring assets, even more forms are required along with recent statement copies of the assets being moved.

Many clients will be asked to sign stacks and stacks of paper depending on how many accounts they have. It can be daunting, most certainly. The good news is that your advisor or his or her staff will likely do the bulk of the paperwork for you. That being said, you do have a responsibility to yourself to understand what you are signing and why. And for more good news, most likely the paperwork is the same for each type of account you are opening, but that doesn't mean you shouldn't review it. First of all, you don't want any surprises in the aftermath, and secondly, you do want to make sure the advisor has accurately represented your personal information.

If you are having assets transferred from one custodian to another, it can take one to two weeks, providing there are no problems. Difficulty can be encountered if there are titling issues, errors on the paperwork, or if the accompanying statement is older than 90 days. If you had been working with an advisor who is listed as the registered representative, don't be surprised to receive a telephone call from him attempting to save the account.

QUICK TIPS

- Understand any agreements signed as well as custodial arrangements, fees, reporting, and so on.
- Verify your information is accurately represented on all paperwork.
- Furnish the chosen advisor with detailed information about your situation, goals and objectives, as well as any foreseen obstacles and/or opportunities.
- Come to terms with your own risk tolerance.

Chapter 16

Maintenance of the Advisor–Client Relationship

Hopefully, the advisor has laid out for you what you can expect once all of the planning has been done, investment direction has been agreed upon, paperwork completed, and assets transferred in regard to what should happen with communications and meetings as time goes on. If not, be sure to clarify what you can anticipate going forward and what is expected of you as the client. Again it could differ depending on whether you are doing financial planning, asset management, or purchasing products like investments or insurance. In all cases, major changes in your own situation, such as a death or disability of a family member, inheritance, goal attainment, marriage, divorce, and so on, warrant at the very least a review of plans put into place. These nonregular reviews will have to be initiated by you as your advisor is not likely to know about such situations unless you give him or her a heads up.

- **Financial Planning:** Can be a one-shot deal where a plan is done and a fee is paid or as an ongoing process. You should review your own plan at least once a year to see where you are relative to your goal(s). If you are way off the mark, then it might make sense to reengage the advisor. As your time frame tightens, you should also be revisiting your plan more frequently.

- **Insurance Purchase:** Should be reviewed on an annual basis to be sure adequate coverage is in place as well as to verify that you are not paying for too much insurance or overpaying for what you have. For insurance that is based on factors such as age and health, most likely you will not be able to purchase less expensive coverage, though it is possible as insurance companies can adjust premiums based on their experience with claims. Whole life insurance should be reviewed annually to be sure that cash values and dividends are supporting the death benefit as originally planned. Sometimes changes in interest rates, mortality rates, and dividends can affect how whole or universal life insurance performs. Insurance companies do issue annual statements that should be reviewed. If you don't understand the statement, be sure to call your advisor as you don't want to find out too late that the program did not perform as predicted. This is especially true with any variable insurance contract or annuity that you own. A variable contract's performance is based on the value of the underlying investments or sub-accounts, which are very similar to mutual funds and can go down or up depending on what is happing in various markets. If the sub-accounts are underperforming, the whole contract could be put in jeopardy. Thus, variable contracts should be looked at quarterly (insurance companies typically issue statements for these types of accounts on a quarterly basis) and a conversation, even if only by telephone, makes sense on the annual anniversary to make sure all of the moving parts are functioning properly to provide you with appropriate benefits.

- **Investment Purchases:** Depend on the various markets with which you are investing and your time frame. You should look at your statements on a quarterly basis and understand any fluctuations in values and whether your performance relative to the appropriate markets (bond, stock, international, and so on) is reasonable. Share amounts can change if dividends and capital gains are being reinvested. Go over your investments with your advisor at least annually. If changes are recommended, be sure to understand why and what new costs you could incur. Keep in mind that the advisor might be compensated for making changes; thus, you should be certain that adjustments are made in your best interest and not just fattening the wallet of the advisor. Over time it is likely that your portfolio will need to be rebalanced. As certain asset classes perform well and others don't, your original asset allocation can become skewed. Rebalancing is a way to systematically take gains from assets that have performed well and make purchases in undervalued investments, bringing the asset allocation in line with your advisor's recommendations. Rebalancing is not always needed but should be looked at twice a year and certainly during times of market volatility. However, the benefits of rebalancing also should be weighed against any costs involved in the way of commissions and taxes that might need to be paid on any realized gains from appreciated assets upon a sale.

- **Assets Under Management:**   Are presumably actively watched by your advisor. Most advisors will meet face-to face with clients on an annual basis or more depending on how complicated the situation is, the level of assets under management, and possibly how much volatility the markets in which you are investing are experiencing. Depending on whether or not your advisor has discretionary authority (the ability to make changes without client notification), you might or might not hear from her when she feels changes need to be made. If she does not have discretionary authority, she will be in touch regarding changes that need to be made including any rebalancing that needs to be done. Unlike advisors who receive a commission, a change in a managed account should not cost you additional fees under most circumstances except a possible ticket charge, though many advisors do cover these costs for their managed clients through the fee that is paid to them.

Your advisor might also provide a variety of other communications from financial planning newsletters, market discussions, and specialty statements as well as emailed updates and information. In regard to electronic communications, be careful not to email full account numbers, social security numbers, or any other personal identification. Most firms have policies in this regard that apply to their advisors as a measure to help protect clients and their assets.

QUICK TIPS

- Ask the advisor what regular communications you can expect.
- Be sure to inform the advisor about any major changes in your life that could affect your finances.

Chapter 17

Activity

When it comes to financial programs and products, activity can be beneficial but also can be detrimental to the growth of your financial investments. Activity can sometimes be used as a synonym for the word *churning* (excessive trading of investment products). If you are a purchaser of fixed or variable life insurance, fixed or variable annuities, other types of insurance, mutual funds, stocks, bonds, and/or other investment products and your advisor regularly recommends replacing your existing programs with others similar to what you already own, it is possible he or she is participating in the practice of churning. Churning is an unethical activity employed by some advisors to increase earned commissions; thus, it does not apply to assets under management, portfolio development, and financial planning that are done on a fee only basis as commissions shouldn't come into play under these scenarios.

Though the term is typically used to describe excessive trading of investment products—stocks, bonds, mutual funds, exchange traded funds, and so on—it is not unheard of in regard to insurance-based programs, which would be insurance and annuities. Keep in mind that insurance products can pay significant commissions to those who sell them; thus, if a replacement is recommended to you, be sure you understand any costs that will affect benefits and cash values, as well as how premiums and your benefits will change. If the insurance purchase involves any health-related underwriting, do not surrender your old policy until the new one is in place in the event you do not qualify for the new coverage as expected.

Churning in an investment account is a violation of federal and state securities laws and most frequently applies to accounts over which the advisor has control as well as discretionary authority. Typical investment churning involves the excessive trading of shares of stocks, though other commissionable investment products could be traded more frequently than necessary, resulting in commissions for the advisor. This is another good reason why you should check your statements each month and any trade confirmations that come in. Normal activity that you will see on your statements will include capital gain and dividend distributions. Frequently these types of distributions are reinvested, so this type of activity would not constitute churning. Be sure you understand the purpose behind any trades that are done in your account and what costs are associated. If it appears that investments are being turned over more frequently than originally discussed based on your investment objective and the types of investments being used, it might be time to speak with the advisor to clarify the account objectives, and why frequent trading is occurring and what it is costing you. If your questions are not answered in a way that is satisfactory, you might want to consider speaking with the advisor's manager or supervisor or OSJ (Office of Supervisory Jurisdiction).

Inactivity can also be a problem and could be an indication that you are being neglected as a client. In most years you wouldn't expect major changes to fixed types of insurance and annuities, though they still should be reviewed to determine whether or not they are performing as expected. Variable insurance and annuities can sometimes be set up to be automatically rebalanced at regular intervals, but again the programs should be reviewed for performance purposes and adjusted if necessary. Depending on the size and purpose of your investment account, you most likely should expect some change throughout any given year. If there haven't been any efforts to update and/or rebalance your account, you should ask why, especially if your account is being actively managed. If you are instead paying on a commission basis, keep in mind that a change could cost you; thus, the advisor may be trying to keep your own costs down if change is not dire. Also keep in mind that investment changes can often trigger tax consequences. If your sales price is higher than your purchase price, you would be responsible for capital gains on federal and state levels on the difference if the trade occurs in a taxable account. Thus, an advisor might be making changes in your nontaxable accounts to complement and avoid triggering realized gains in a taxable account. Often advisors will look for ways to trigger losses as you can currently use capital losses to offset capital gains and deduct up to $3,000 per year in losses. However, a loss is a loss, and unless the advisor reinvests the proceeds, you are unlikely to make up for the loss over time.

QUICK TIPS

- Ask about how much activity is expected for the types of programs you own.
- Understand how activity is represented on any communications provided to you and what costs are involved with any changes.

Chapter 18

Accessibility

Your ability to communicate with your advisor is key to your own financial success. It is important that you understand how you and your advisor will best communicate: in person, via the telephone, through email, by traditional mail, or a combination of these mediums. As an advisor, I find email is a great way to communicate and maintain documentation of action items although investment orders cannot be given over email or voicemail and not all of my clients even have email. I also find email to be impersonal at times, and I like to talk with clients on the telephone because I can get more of a sense of their moods and how they are doing. During my face-to-face meetings, I feel we accomplish the most, typically because this is dedicated time to go over the big picture, and I can tune into all nonverbal cues and see how they are physically doing. Thus, I find different purposes for the various communication methods, and I do try to key into how my various clients prefer to communicate with me, as well.

Along with agreeing how you will communicate, you should get a sense of how frequently communications should occur and under what circumstances. Some advisors have a casual, open door policy; others have a more rigid communication schedule. Though regular contact is important, there are times when getting in touch should be a priority. For the advisor, it is during times of extreme market volatility, whether or not portfolio changes need to be made. For the client, it is in regard to any major change in circumstances. I know often clients feel they don't want to bother their advisors, but they cannot guide you if you don't let them know about changes that occur in your life.

QUICK TIPS

- Ask about your advisor's communications policy.
- Develop a communications plan that suits both you and the advisor.
- Inform your advisor about changes in your life which affect your finances either directly or circuitously.

Chapter 19

The Dysfunctional Relationship

There are many symptoms that could indicate that you are in a dysfunctional relationship with your advisor. Some are minor, though if combined with a number of small offenses could warrant taking action on your part. They could also be indications of larger problems and are worth tracking and/or questioning. There are also major symptoms that typically call for more aggressive action. Whether an occurrence is big or small, don't do nothing and hope that things will get better. If something happens (or doesn't) happen that annoys you, bring it to your advisor's attention. Most financial professionals who are serious about their clients and their businesses will take any criticism as an opportunity to learn how they and their staff can better serve you and the rest of their clients.

Items to pay attention to include

- Not receiving account statements on a regular basis
- Lack of regular communication
- Unresponsiveness to service requests
- No follow-through on agreed upon actions
- Chronically unavailable status
- Delays in return telephone calls
- Misinterpretation of client-oriented directives
- Inaccuracies on paperwork, financial plans, or other communications
- Errors in trading or other transactions

Errors, especially in regard to trading, are usually more serious than some of the communication-related oversights. In the event there is a trading error, be sure to understand whether or not you were "harmed" in any way; in other words did you lose money or miss out on potential gains, and if so how does the advisor plan to fix the error? In regard to service and communication problems, do bring items to your advisor's attention but also keep track of items of annoyance. If the same problem is chronic or issues continue to pile up, you need to know when to cut your losses and move to someone who is attentive to and appreciative of having you as a client.

More serious problems require more aggressive action, such as getting the advisor's manager or Office of Supervisory Jurisdiction (OSJ), the compliance department of the advisor's broker/dealer, and/or even state or federal securities regulators involved. Areas of concern can include

- **Breach of Contract:**   Arises typically out of a conflict with account applications and agreements. These forms require the advisor to handle client accounts in accordance with the rules and regulations of the securities industry. Mismanagement and/or failure to follow customers' instructions are sometimes triggers of a breach of contract claim.

- **Churning:**   Occurs when there is excessive trading of securities within an account where the broker benefits in commission gains. Churning can be measured with the turnover ratio—in other words, how many times has the portfolio been "turned over" within a 12-month period and/or using equity to cost ratios.

- **Misrepresentation or Fraud:**   A client is damaged due to the reliance of the customer on the advisor's representation or omission of material information.

- **Negligence:**   Violation of the advisor's duty to exercise care of a client's account such as providing a properly diversified account.

- **Unsuitability:** Breach of the Financial Industry Regulatory Authority's requirement of registered representatives to know their customers. In other words, their recommendations and implementation actions need to be in line with their client's financial condition, level of knowledge about investing, risk tolerance, and investment objectives.

If you suspect your advisor's actions or lack of action fall into one of these categories, you should contact the advisors manager/OSJ and/or compliance department or seek legal council depending on how severe the violation is. Though regulators are sympathetic to the investing public, if you do not have a realistic claim, shelling out a lot of money to lawyers can add insult to injury and might not be the best route to go for resolution.

With minor and major errors and violations in mind, you can hopefully spot whether or not you are stuck in a dysfunctional relationship with your advisor. Because this is a relationship that is personal, it can be difficult to extract yourself from it because there is a good possibility that you actually like your advisor as a person. He's probably acted as your confidant, sounding board, and/or has been a resource of information for you. Regardless of how you feel toward this person emotionally, if he is not handling you and your finances with the diligence you deserve, it is either time to have a heart to heart or to just get out and move on. (Hopefully, you still have that list of advisors you prepared during your financial professional search so that you don't have to start from square one.)

There are three categories of advisors who create problems for clients, though they can have similar characteristics in each situation. In so many cases, they are extremely likable and get by with inappropriate handling of accounts via their "winning" personality. Clients may let things slide because they don't want to create any tension in the relationship or the inadequate advisor is able to distract the client from realizing things are not as they should be. The advisor might be like Bernard Madoff whose secrecy and aloofness about his investment management strategies made clients feel privileged to be among the select few doing business with him and did not want to upset the apple cart by asking too many questions. In fact, according to Mr. Madoff's former secretary, his managed clients frequently complained about a lack of customer service from his staff. Or an advisor could be like my ex-husband, Bradford Bleidt, who would seemingly do anything for his beloved clients in hopes they wouldn't catch on to what was actually going on. Again, these are the extreme situations, but there are variations on the themes among those who put their own interests ahead of their clients. There are basically three types of advisors who employ abusive practices and with whom you want to avoid or sever a professional relationship:

- **The Thief:** Like Bernard Madoff and Bradford Bleidt, the thief is an advisor who illegally uses client assets for purposes not intended by the client and typically for the advisor's own gain.

- **The Egoist:** An advisor who might not be out-and-out stealing from clients but makes recommendations based on his or her best interests and not necessarily those of clients. Examples include financial professionals who frequently recommend portfolio changes in order to gain additional commissions or those who persuade clients to purchase unnecessary or unsuitable products because of their own potential compensation.

- **The Incompetent:** An advisor who is not qualified to deliver proper recommendations or carry them out. Such an individual might have the best of intentions to provide proper care and services to clients but lack enough experience and training to do so efficiently and accurately. Other incompetent advisors might lack the drive and conscientiousness that is required to consistently service clients thoroughly.

QUICK TIPS

- Pay attention to your own feelings of satisfaction.
- Bring problem items to the attention of your advisor and see how he or she reacts.
- Evaluate the seriousness of any issue to determine the level of resolution you need.

Chapter 20

Criminal Versus Non-Criminal Behavior

Those who put themselves out there as financial professionals who are actually participating in criminal behavior are not going to be easy to spot as their illicit activities are likely to be well covered. Hopefully, you now have the tools to keep your hard earned assets away from any situation that may seem peculiar, and you are certainly better off safe than sorry. Pay attention to the red flags discussed such as avoiding financial professionals who

- Cannot adequately show you where your assets will be held and in what ways they will or will not be protected.
- Provide ambiguous explanations about potential investment strategies.
- Promise unrealistically high and/or consistent rates of return.
- Represent unregistered investments.
- Avoid providing you with a reasonable explanation about how they get paid and applicable costs affecting your situation.
- Furnish information verbally or through brochures or other sales materials that is inconsistent or in conflict with other available information, such as what is published on the websites of the SEC and FINRA.
- Do not provide appropriate documentation for your authorization.
- Have a disturbing disciplinary history with FINRA, the SEC, or any other professional organization to which they belong or once belonged.

- Make you feel uncomfortable because they are pushy or aloof.

Those participating in criminal behavior could try to lure you into a number of different schemes often disguised in various ways. Electronic means have made it easier for investment schemes and fraudulent advisors to flourish through email and clever web design. It is much easier for schemers to get the word out about their programs and in doing so present a professional image via a well-designed website. Knowing what to look for in such communications and websites will help keep you closer to your cash. Approach any potential investment pitch with a skeptical front. Make the assumption that it is a scam until you are proven otherwise. As an investment professional, I have had clients run "ideas" past me due to a letter or an email that was sent to them by someone they didn't know. Though the Internet has made it easier for fraudsters to promote their schemes, it has also facilitated the ability to look into them. In many cases it is clear something is wrong as soon as you visit the scheme's website as it is unlikely to have any of the required disclosure verbiage required for the sale of registered investments. There will be no mention of a prospectus or any other traditional documentation involved with the sale of securities. To legitimize themselves, fraudsters will frequently be happy to send you contact information of "existing investors." Should you speak with them, they are likely to tout the benefits of the investment they have made. Keep in mind you are probably speaking with a member of the fraudster's entourage or an early investor who has not yet realized she is participating in a scheme.

Remaining skeptical doesn't only keep you closer to your cash, but it can also keep you out of trouble. A highly educated, very intelligent friend of mine was successfully lured into a Ponzi scheme that promoted the high returns of short-term foreign bank note trading. She mentioned it in passing, noting that it was a coworker she trusted and respected who had recommended it to her. As she was not in the investment field, I offered to check it out for her. She declined my offer, suggesting that the person who got her involved wanted to keep things under wraps. Apparently things went well, so much so that she pulled money out of her retirement account to invest, incurring a bit of a tax burden along the way and even inviting me to join her, which I declined, again suggesting I would check it out for her. Eventually the scheme collapsed, and regulators got involved. She actually ended up being found responsible for luring in other investors and had to pay a hefty fine.

Keep in mind that though fraudulent investing schemes tend to follow similar patterns, they are often dressed up and disguised in very creative ways to throw off savvy individuals. The promotions I have seen recently for such scams vary greatly from gift giving promotions that even claim you can take a tax deduction, to investment loans, oil and gas drilling programs, and so on. However, they usually follow similar themes:

- **Ponzi:** Most recently popularized by Bernard Madoff, a Ponzi scheme is one in which the "advisor" collects investment dollars from victims promising unobtainable returns (either unrealistically high or in the case of Mr. Madoff, consistent). The schemer pays off earlier investors with the deposits of new investors. A Ponzi scheme will collapse when the pool of assets is depleted due to the spending habits of the schemer, lack of new investors, and/or poor returns of invested assets. Ponzi schemes can flourish among social and religious groups because of the referral nature of the recruiting program. Satisfied investors become natural promoters of the fraudster, typically a member of the network, among their peers. This was true of Bernard Madoff among the Jewish community as well as Bradford Bleidt as a member of the Masons.

- **Pyramid:** A pyramid scheme relies on the recruitment of new investors. You are typically asked to make a small investment and then recruit others to be part of the investment program. As you recruit others and they in turn bring on more people, the promoted rate of return on your investment skyrockets. The scheme continues until there are not enough recruits to support investors as the scheme literally runs out of potential participants. As the base of the pyramid crumbles, only those at the top of the pyramid receive any return on their investment, and the vast majority of investors lose.

- **Multi-level Marketing:** Though there are legitimate multi-level marketing companies such as Amway, Avon, and Mary Kay, the same approach can be used to disguise a scam. The legitimate companies work because investors not only sell products that are bought by customers outside of the company, but investors are also encouraged to recruit salespeople to sell additional products on which they will make a commission. With a multi-level marketing scheme, the product being sold has no actual value outside of the scam, such as a marketing list, so no one would actually buy the product unless he or she were being recruited into the scheme itself.

- **Chain Letters:** The Internet has certainly facilitated the production of chain letters—that is for sure! The letters themselves are not illegal until money comes into play. Many of these letters request you send a nominal amount to one or more persons on a list, remove the top name, add your's to the bottom of the list, and forward the letter to a number of people. Theoretically, your name would be moved up the list until you become the beneficiary, and the more people you send letters to, supposedly the more money will come your way. Even if it were legal, think it through: There is nothing to ensure that those further down the line from you will send you the suggested amount if anything. They can simply add their names without paying anyone. You also have to think about what you would end up investing in copies and postage. It's just not worth it, and again, it is illegal when money becomes a part of it.

- **Offshore:**   Incentives promoted to invest offshore usually include higher returns, favorable tax treatment, and protection from creditors, including ex-spouses. Promoters tout the benefits of investing in corporations registered outside of the United States for the purposes of creating tax free returns. The problem with offshore investing is the lack of regulation and the ability for U.S. enforcement agencies to protect investors and assist those who are harmed. Many victims of offshore investing scams are intelligent, educated, and well read but not necessarily wealthy. They are lured in by elaborate presentations promising them benefits that don't exist.

- **Pump and Dump:**   Fraudsters promote the attributes of a thinly traded public corporation in which they already have a substantial holding using exaggerated and misleading advertising done via cold calling and/or the Internet. The process is usually used with micro and small cap stocks and artificially increases the value of the shares at which point the scammers dump their investment with a nice profit, leaving victims with unrecoverable losses.

Investment scammers are successful because they use your emotions against you. It does not matter how well-educated you are or how much investment experience you have. We are all susceptible when we allow our emotions to overcome common sense. Certainly most investment scams start with the promise of high and/or guaranteed returns, tapping into our own greed and need for safety. Always keep in mind that risk and return are highly correlated; thus, guarantees paired with the promise of returns higher than that of bank CDs cannot coexist. After all, even some money market investments dipped below their consistent one dollar per share value during the

2008 banking crisis. Once scammers capture your interest by tapping into your greed factor, they use several other techniques to reel you in. They may inspire you to act quickly and without proper investigation by imposing short time frames or claiming that only a limited number of investors can get in on the deal. Do not fall for these high pressure tactics. If you are unable to perform your own due diligence within your own time, the investment is not worth your hard earned dollars. Some fraudsters will give you the time to do you own investigation, but they'll also provide you with their own tools such as referrals and testimonials from existing investors. Unless you perform your own investigation independent from anything offered by the salespeople, you are unlikely to get the truth about the opportunity. Anyone with whom you speak is likely to be in on the scam or is already a victim and just doesn't realize it yet.

QUICK TIPS

- Know where your assets are and how they are protected.
- Don't accept ambiguous explanations.
- Be wary of inconsistencies.
- Do not fall prey to pushy personalities.
- Be skeptical of promises that are "too good to be true."
- Familiarize yourself with the various patterns investment schemes tend to follow.

Chapter 21

Filing a Complaint

Should you suspect you are being solicited by someone in a fraudulent manner, you can file a complaint or tip with the Financial Industry Regulatory Authority (FINRA) at www.finra.org or:

FINRA Complaints and Tips

9509 Key West Avenue

Rockville, MD 20850

Phone: (301) 590-6500

Fax: (866) 397-3290

Or with the Securities and Exchange Commission at www.sec.gov:

SEC Complaint Center

100 F Street NE

Washington, DC 20549-0213

Phone: (202) 551-6551

Fax: (703) 813-6965

Or the North American Securities Administrators Association to find your state's regulator at www.nasaa.org:

North American Securities Administrators Association, Inc. (NASAA)

750 First Street, N.E., Suite 1140

Washington, DC 20002

Phone: (202) 737-0900

Fax: (202) 783-3571

Though they are not necessarily easy to detect, once uncovered, investment scams are fairly black and white when it comes to determining whether or not an illegal activity has occurred. There are other offenses that are not as clear and fall into a gray area. Investors may not be aware that they are being taken advantage of because there hasn't been obvious misappropriation of their funds, and the only clues may be disappointing investment returns. According to FINRA, you should be aware that certain types of conduct in the securities industry are prohibited, including the following:[1]

1. Recommending to a customer the purchase or sale of a security that is unsuitable given the customer's age, financial situation, investment objective, and investment experience. Investment in a particular type of security may be unsuitable, or the amount or frequency of transactions may be excessive and therefore unsuitable for a given customer.

2. Purchasing or selling securities in a customer's account without first contacting the customer and the customer did not specifically authorize the sale or purchase, unless the broker has received from the customer written discretionary authority to effect transactions in the account or the broker was given discretion as to price and time.

3. Switching a customer from one mutual fund to another when there is no legitimate investment purpose underlying the switch.

4. Misrepresenting or failing to disclose material facts concerning an investment. Examples of information that may be considered material and that should be accurately presented to customers include: the risks of investing in a particular

---

[1] © 2009 FINRA. All rights reserved. FINRA is a registered trademark of the Financial Industry Regulatory Authority, Inc. Reprinted with permission from FINRA.

security; the charges or fees involved; company financial information; and technical or analytical information; such as bond ratings.

5. Removing funds or securities from a customer's account without the customer's prior authorization.

6. Charging a customer excessive markups, markdowns, or commissions on the purchase or sale of securities.

7. Guaranteeing customers that they will not lose money on a particular securities transaction, making specific price predictions, or agreeing to share in any losses in the customer's account.

8. Private securities transactions between a broker and a customer that may violate NASD rules, particularly where such transactions are done without the knowledge and permission of the sales representative's firm.

9. Trading for a firm's account in preference to a customer by trading ahead of a customer limit order, absent a valid exception.

10. Failure by a market maker to display a customer limit order in its published quotes, absent a valid exception.

11. Failing to use reasonable diligence to see that a customer's order is executed at the best possible price, given prevailing market conditions.

12. Purchasing or selling a security while in possession of material, nonpublic information regarding an issuer.

13. Using any manipulative, deceptive, or other fraudulent device or contrivance to effect any transaction in or induce the purchase or sale of any security.

If you have a complaint about a broker's conduct, first ask the individual involved about the situation. If you are not satisfied with any explanation provided, get in touch with the broker's manager and compliance department. If you suspect you have been financially harmed, be sure all of your correspondence is in writing and you maintain a copy of all correspondence and documentation, such as trade tickets and statements, pertaining to the situation.

If you are unable to obtain a resolution, you might then want to consider filing a complaint with FINRA, the SEC, and/or your state's securities division. You might also want to retain an attorney at this point and one who specializes in securities law. Keep in mind, however, there is risk involved with investing, and the sole fact that your investments have decreased in value might not be enough to make a satisfactory claim against a broker and/or his firm.

A complaint should be filed in writing and contain

- The name of the broker (or brokers) and the name of his or her firm and/or broker/dealer if different along with appropriate addresses and telephone numbers
- A description of the conduct about which you are complaining, including the names and symbols (if applicable) of any specific investments that were involved
- A detailed description of the conduct involved including any applicable dates
- A copy of any relevant documentation such as statements, trade confirmations, and correspondence
- Your contact information including address, telephone numbers, and email addresses

Once FINRA receives your complaint, staff members determine whether an investigation should be opened and might request documents and information from the applicable brokerage firm and its employees. You should be prepared to speak with FINRA staff members, provide information, sign a sworn statement, and potentially testify at a disciplinary hearing if one is conducted. FINRA can close the investigation without taking any disciplinary action. Inaction, however, has no bearing on any arbitration or mediation proceedings. Certain complaints may be referred to other private securities regulators, the

SEC, and/or federal or state enforcement agencies for further action and possibly criminal prosecution.

FINRA offers dispute resolution processes consisting of mediation and arbitration, which can be a quicker, more convenient, and less expensive means to settling a dispute than heading to court. The purpose behind mediation is to facilitate the communication and negotiation of a resolution between disputing parties through the use of an impartial mediator. The mediation process can consist of face-to-face discussions between the conflicting parties and/or utilization of the mediator as a go-between to carry out the negotiation. Approximately 80% of professionally mediated cases have been settled.

Arbitration is a more formal approach to resolving a dispute and can take place in the event mediation fails or is not an option. Most firms have an arbitration agreement attached to the New Account Form, which is completed when an account is established. Utilization of legal counsel is recommended. Impartial arbitrators are selected by FINRA to hear cases and might or might not have a securities background. Potential arbitrators must submit profiles, demonstrating their knowledge of the financial industry and issues around investing.

After your claim is filed with FINRA, you will need to sign a Submission Agreement, which binds you to the arbitration outcome and submit a nonrefundable filing fee (a fee calculator is provided on FINRA's website). The claim is then served to the "respondent." If your claim is less than $25,000, it is provided to the arbitrator along with the respondent's answer. The arbitrator will review the statements and all supporting materials and make a decision based on what he or she has read. You can also request a live hearing.

In cases involving more than $25,000 or if requested, a hearing will be scheduled. Organization is important when it comes to an arbitration hearing as the decision-making individuals appreciate information that is clear, concise, and presented efficiently. You are responsible for preparing yourself, any witnesses, and evidence for the hearing sessions as well as notifying the other party identifying those testifying on your behalf. You also must submit copies of any evidence 20 calendar days in advance and bring with you enough copies for each arbitrator as well as one for the file.

Each party participates in the selection process of the arbitrators and can randomly eliminate up to four of the potential choices without reason. The arbitrators will determine the format of the hearing, but will generally swear in the parties, allow each party to make his presentation and counterclaim, allow for cross-examination of witnesses, as well as give each party the opportunity to make closing statements. You should be prepared for a cross-examine situation and to answer questions posed by the arbitrators. A decision from the arbitrators should come within 30 days, and any payments determined to be due are to be paid within 30 days of that decision. Keep in mind that the arbitration process is one that is both public and binding.

Quick Tips

- Understand the level of seriousness of any complaint you have and whether or not it is valid.
- Seek resolution of any matter with your advisor and his or her firm first.
- Be sure to follow recommended procedure when filing a complaint with a securities regulatory entity.

Appendix A

Consumer Resources

There are a plethora of useful resources available to consumers to assist them with their financial planning and investing, but apparent resources can sometimes be, in reality, sales presentations or even window dressing for a scam. This is true of email or spam you may receive, seminars, luncheons, dinners, websites, mail, and telephone solicitations. If information is coming your way via an entity with which you are not familiar, approach it with a healthy dose of skepticism.

Most material is available on the websites of the various organizations, though some entities provide access to information via the telephone and/or through mailed requests. Keep in mind that some of these resources are associations that do require the payment of dues for access to some information.

The **Alliance for Investor Education (AIE)** provides soup to nuts investor education resources covering mutual funds, stocks, futures, financial planning, scams, as well as links to other resources. The AIE also provides events for investors:

www.investoreducation.org

The **American Association of Individual Investors (AAII)** provides newsletters, stock market information, investor conferences, member interaction, as well as resources for investing and doing financial planning:

> www.aaii.com
>
> (800) 428-2244
>
> 625 N Michigan Avenue
>
> Chicago, IL 60611

The **American Association of Retired Persons (AARP)** publishes information on retirement and estate planning, investing, insurances, consumer fraud, Social Security, and lifestyle issues:

> www.aarp.org
>
> (888) OUR-AARP
>
> 601 E Street NW
>
> Washington, DC 20049

The **American Financial Services Association Education Foundation (AFSAEF)** strives to increase consumer awareness in the area of personal financial responsibility through educational resources in the areas of money management, credit, and other resources to improve financial literacy:

> www.afsaef.org
>
> (202) 466-8611
>
> 919 18th Street NW, Suite 300
>
> Washington, DC 20006-5517

The **American Institute for Certified Public Accountants (AICPA)** provides resources to assist the consumer in finding a CPA, identifying CPAs with disciplinary histories, as well as some financial planning resources:

> www.aicpa.org
>
> (888) 777-7077
>
> 220 Leigh Farm Road
>
> Durham, NC 27707

The **Board of Governors of the Federal Reserve** provides consumer information on scams, mortgages and financing, credit, banks, personal finance, as well as federal agency contacts:

> www.federalreserve.gov

The **Certified Financial Planner Board of Standards, Inc.** is a resource for information about financial planning, learning about financial professionals, finding an advisor, filing a complaint about a CERTIFIED FINANCIAL PLANNER™ professional, and learning about disciplinary histories of specific CFP® practitioners:

> www.cfp.net
>
> (800) 487-1497
>
> 1425 K Street NW, Suite 500
>
> Washington, DC 20005

The **CFA Institute** provides investor educational articles as well as information about the Chartered Financial Analyst designation and program:

> www.cfainstitute.org
>
> (800) 247-8132

The **Consumer Federation of America** is an advocacy, research, education, and service organization that provides information on various topics including finance. Resources are available in the areas of banking, credit and debt, insurance, and investing:

> www.consumerfed.org
>
> (202) 387-6121
>
> 1620 I Street NW, Suite 200
>
> Washington, DC 20006

The **Federal Deposit Insurance Corporation (FDIC)** provides information for consumers on financial matters, banks and banking, identity theft and privacy, real estate and housing, as well as FDIC coverage:

> www.fdic.gov
>
> (877) ASK-FDIC

The **Federal Trade Commission's Bureau of Consumer Protection** provides educational publications, consumer resources, and information on filing a complaint:

> www.ftc.gov
>
> (202) 326-3300
>
> Federal Trade Commission
>
> 600 Pennsylvania Avenue NW
>
> Washington, DC 20580

The **Financial Industry Regulatory Authority (FINRA)** offers everything from investing and some financial planning education, broker check resources, a "scam meter," and other information on fraudulent practices to claim filing procedures:

> www.finra.org
>
> (301) 590-6500
>
> 1735 K Street
>
> Washington, DC 20006

The **Financial Planning Association (FPA)**'s website has pages designed specifically for the public covering various financial planning topics as well as the ability to ask questions and find a potential planner via the website:

> www.fpa.net
>
> (800) 322-4237
>
> 1600 K Street NW, Suite 201
>
> Washington, DC 20006

The **Foundation for Investor Education** has information on various planning topics and investing as well as newsletters and material on working with a financial professional:

> www.pathtoinvesting.org
>
> SIFMA Foundation for Investor Education
>
> 120 Broadway, 35th Floor
>
> New York, NY 10271

The **Investment Company Institute (ICI)** focuses on mutual funds and investment companies and issues consumer materials on these topics:

> www.ici.org
>
> (202) 326-5800
>
> 1401 H Street NW, Suite 1200
>
> Washington, DC 20005

The **Investment Management Consultants Association (IMCA)** has financial calculators, a planner search mechanism, information about designations, member disciplinary history, as well as a complaint area:

> www.imca.org
>
> (303) 770-3377
>
> 5619 DTC Parkway, Suite 500
>
> Greenwood Village, CO 80111

The **Investor Protector Trust** publishes financial education information and provides resources for those interested in teaching about finances:

> www.investorprotection.org
>
> (202) 775-2112
>
> 919 18th Street NW, Suite 300
>
> Washington, DC 20006-5517

The **National Association of Insurance Commissioners (NAIC)** provides information for consumers, including those with atypical circumstances such as military involvement and those with domestic partners. The NAIC can also put consumers in touch with their own local division of insurance:

> www.naic.org
>
> (866) 470-NAIC
>
> NAIC Central Office
>
> 2301 McGee Street, Suite 800
>
> Kansas City, MO 64108-2662

The **National Association of Investors Corporation** is member-driven and provides investor education as well as various calculators and online tools:

> www.betterinvesting.org
>
> (877) 275-6242
>
> PO Box 220
>
> Royal Oak, MI 48068

The **National Endowment for Financial Education (NEFE)** has material on financial planning topics as well as information on potential free assistance:

> www.nefe.org
>
> (303) 741-6333
>
> 5299 DTC Boulevard, Suite 1300
>
> Greenwood Village, CO 80111

The **National Foundation for Credit Counseling (NFCC)** provides budget worksheets, financial calculators, consumer tips, and information on housing, credit, bankruptcy, and financial matters as well as a Credit Counselor search mechanism:

> www.nfcc.org
>
> (800) 388-2227
>
> 801 Roeder Road, Suite 900
>
> Silver Spring, MD 20910

The **New York Stock Exchange (NYSE)** has market and investment data as well as consumer information on a number of topics including asset transfers, broker change of affiliation, and margin accounts:

> www.nyse.com
>
> (212) 656-3000
>
> 11 Wall Street
>
> New York, NY 10005

The **North American Securities Administrators Association (NASAA)** has its own fraud center, investor alerts and tips, as well as information on how to contact your own local regulatory authority:

> www.nasaa.org

The **Securities Industry and Financial Markets Association** is a resource for bond investing. The association offers bond market information, calculators, and headlines as well as consumer education on the various bond markets and investing in fixed income:

> www.investinginbonds.com

The **Securities Investor Protection Corporation (SIPC)** provides education on SIPC coverage, information on member firms, claim processing explanations, and updates on various cases in process:

> www.sipc.org
>
> (202) 371-8300
>
> 805 15th Street NW, Suite 800
>
> Washington, DC 20005-2215

The **Social Security Administration (SSA)** provides information on Social Security benefits as well as Medicare. They also provide a mechanism to report fraud and abuse:

> www.ssa.gov
>
> (800) 772-1213
>
> Office of Public Inquiries
>
> Windsor Park Building
>
> 6401 Security Boulevard
>
> Baltimore, MD 21235

The **U.S. Department of the Treasury** promotes financial education through the Financial Literacy and Education Commission:

> www.treas.gov and/or www.mymoney.gov
>
> (202) 622-2000 or (888) MyMoney
>
> 1500 Pennsylvania Avenue NW
>
> Washington, DC 20220

The **U.S. Securities and Exchange Commission (SEC)** provides a means to check out brokers and advisors, educational publications, various calculators, information on investor claims and regulatory matters, as well as lists of unregistered soliciting entities that are subject to complaints and fictitious governmental agencies and international organizations:

www.sec.gov

(800) SEC-0330

100 F Street NE

Washington, DC 20549

Credit Ratings Agencies

A.M. Best is a worldwide credit rating agency that serves the financial and insurance industries. Best's credit ratings are independent opinions regarding the reliability of a financial institution. The ratings tell the consumer if an institution is dependable enough to be given credit or to be lent money. The ratings are based on a complete assessment of the company's balance sheet strength, operating performance, and if applicable, the details of debt securities. Best's scale is a standard A–F letter grade scale.

www.ambest.com

(908) 439-2200

Fitch Ratings, Ltd. uses the same ratings scale as S&P. This ratings company is known worldwide and like the other ratings companies determines the financial risk of entities issuing debt. Its specialties include credit information and analytical tools to help others watch the changes in the ratings and trends. This enables participants to make informed decisions.

www.fitchratings.com

(212) 908-0500

Moody's Investor Services is also a worldwide credit agency specializing in providing information to third parties regarding entity financial risk. They analyze commercial companies and governmental agencies by researching financial reports. They assign a rating based on the following scale: Aaa, Aa1, Aa2, Aa3, A1, A2, A3, Baa1, Baa2, Baa3.

www.moodys.com

(212) 553-1653

Standard and Poor's rating system looks at a company's credit risk of bond issuers from corporations to states, municipalities, and sovereign governments. The rating scale ranges from AAA, AA, A, BBB, BB, B, CCC, to R. If Standard and Poor's thinks that an entity is possibly unstable and they might change future ratings, they will assign the company a plus or minus in addition to the rating:

www.standardandpoors.com

(212) 438-7280

In this age of identity theft and fraud, it doesn't hurt to check your own credit rating on an annual basis to make sure it accurately reflects your situation. Errors can create unpleasant surprises when you go to borrow or refinance; thus, you need to make sure your credit report is mistake-free. You are entitled to one free each year or in the event you feel your identity has been jeopardized. To obtain your free credit report, go to

www.annualcreditreport.com

or call

(877) 322-8228

You will need your name, Social Security number, date of birth, recent addresses, and potentially recent transaction information. You should be able to access the report online immediately or expect it in the mail in 15 days.

You can also go to the major credit agencies themselves, but you might have to pay for the report.

www.equifax.com (800) 685-1111

www.experian.com (714) 830-7000

www.transunion.com (800) 888-4213

In the event you need to dispute an item on your credit report, you will need your ID number with the particular credit agency, name, Social Security number, date of birth, current address, and specifics of the disputed item (company name and account number and the basis for your dispute). This can be done online, by the telephone, or through the mail. You should maintain copies of all materials including any forms completed online. Should you choose to process your dispute on the telephone, be sure to diligently keep notes on the conversation: with whom you spoke and what was said. The credit agency will then contact the company involved with the disputed item and investigate your claim. Should you disagree with the results of the investigation, you have the right to add a 100-word consumer statement that explains your version of the circumstances.

All three companies do provide some consumer educational materials via their websites on fraud, identity theft, and credit.

Appendix B

Glossary

12B-1 Fees
Marketing and distribution fees associated with mutual funds. Both load and no-load funds can have 12B-1 fees associated with them.

ACH
The Automated Clearing House (ACH) network for financial transactions and movement of money from one institution to another.

active portfolio management
A portfolio strategy that utilizes a manager or management team along with available information that seeks to outperform an applicable benchmark or index.

APAM
Allocation Plus Asset Management (APAM) Company was the asset management firm owned by Bradford C. Bleidt.

asset allocation
A strategy involving the utilization of various asset classes in order to reduce risk.

asset management
The use of a professional to collectively oversee a group of investments. The process typically involves the development of an investment policy statement, analysis of existing assets, asset selection, plan implementation, and ongoing monitoring.

back end load
Also known as the Contingent Deferred Sales Charge, a back end load refers to a charge an investor may encounter when redeeming shares of a mutual fund or a variable annuity before a certain time frame has been completed. This charge decreases over time until ultimately reaching zero.

balance sheet
A statement of financial condition showing what is owned, what is owed, and how much owners' equity exists.

balanced mutual fund
A fund that purchases both stocks and bonds with the goal of providing both capital appreciation and income to the investor.

bear
An investor who expects financial markets to go down.

bear market
A market that is trading downward in regard to security prices.

blue sky laws
Laws that vary by state and regulate the offering and sale of securities.

bond
Investment vehicles consisting of debt that are issued by corporations, international, national, state, and municipal governments. An investor in a bond is loaning money to the entity for which he or she will receive interest on the loan and a return of principal after a certain period of time. Bonds trade via markets and can be volatile in nature. Generally, if held until maturity, an investor will receive a return of all her capital, though there can be a risk of default on the bond depending on the financial quality of the issuing entity.

breakpoint
The amount of money a load mutual fund share owner needs to invest in order to qualify for a reduced sales charge.

broker
Someone who executes customer investment orders, either on an institutional basis or for individual customers and is paid a commission. Full service brokers offer advice and generally have access to analytical resources. Discount brokers charge lower commissions than full service brokers but only participate in the execution of client orders and do not usually offer advice or opinions.

bull
An investor who expects a market to participate in an upward trend.

bull market
A market that is trending upward in regard to security prices.

business risk
The risk that a company will not have enough cash flow to meet its operating expenses due to various reasons, but usually economic conditions.

buy on margin
Borrowing off one's security account in order to finance additional securities transactions.

cap
An upper interest rate limit of an adjustable mortgage, equity-index annuity, or a floating rate bond.

capital
The financial assets of a firm or an individual.

capital gain
The difference between the selling price of an asset and the original cost of that asset if it has appreciated in value.

capital loss
The difference between the selling price of an asset and the original cost of that asset if it has depreciated in value.

cash flow
For individuals, cash flow is determined by totaling income and subtracting all expenses. For a potential investment it is an indicator of financial strength.

cash surrender value
The amount an investor in a whole life insurance policy or an annuity will receive if it is cashed in before paying a death benefit.

certificate of deposit (CD)
An instrument used by banks for a specific deposit amount. The deposit will bear a certain interest amount and will mature after a defined time period.

commission
A fee paid to a broker or insurance agent for a transaction. Commissions can be triggered by the purchase or sale of securities or the purchase of insurance products including variable, fixed, equity-index, and immediate annuities.

common stock
Ownership in a corporation represented by shares that are valued by a market. Investments in stock entitle the owner to participate in dividends and vote on corporate matters.

confirmation

A receipt issued upon the execution of a securities trade detailing share amounts and values as well as commissions and fees.

contingent deferred sales charge (CDSC)

Also known as a back end load, the CDSC refers to a charge an investor might encounter when redeeming shares of a mutual fund or a variable annuity before a certain time frame has been completed. This charge decreases over time until ultimately reaching zero.

cost to equity ratio

Calculates the total investment related costs divided by the average equity of a portfolio to determine the rate of return needed for the portfolio to break even.

currency risk

An investment risk term referring to the risk of the movement of various currencies in relation to one another and how it can affect the valuation of an investment. Currency risk comes into play when investors invest in international entities and/or corporations that participate in international business affairs.

custodial fees

Charges assessed by an institution that is in the business of holding securities in safekeeping for investors.

default risk

Assessed by ratings agencies, default risk can also be referred to as credit risk and is the risk that an entity or individual will not be able to meet interest or repayment obligations in regard to a bond or loan.

deferred annuity
A variable or fixed insurance product that allows for the deferral of taxes as the investment grows. Annuities carry little or no life insurance, depending on riders elected by the investor but do receive some beneficial tax treatment provided to life insurance products. Withdrawal of annuity assets is taxed on a last-in, first-out basis. Thus, interest earned is withdrawn first and fully taxable unless the annuity is turned into an income stream (annuitized). The interest also can be subject to a 10% penalty if the contract owner is not yet $59^{1}/_{2}$ years old when it is withdrawn.

defined benefit plan
A retirement pension plan makes defined dollar payments to qualified retirees of an entity. Dollar amounts can be indexed for inflation over the life of the former employee. Benefits cease upon the death of the employee unless an election is made to continue benefits to a spouse.

defined contribution plan
A pension plan that contributes defined dollar amounts to the retirement accounts of entity employees during their time of service and does not guarantee specific payments upon retirement.

discretionary authority
The authorization given to a broker by a client to invest assets without consultation regarding prices, amounts, and security types.

diversification
The investment of funds among various security types that are expected to react differently in varying market conditions with the goal of reducing overall risk within a portfolio.

dividend
A portion of a company's profit paid to owners of both common and preferred stock. Dividends are also paid to the owners of participating whole life insurance policies.

economic risk
The risk associated with the state of an economy and its impact on investments.

emerging markets
The financial markets of developing countries that can involve substantial risk taking but also the possibility of significant returns.

equity
Ownership interest, typically in the form of stock in reference to investing.

ethics
Expected professional conduct standards.

event risk
The risk that some unexpected substantial event will markedly change market pricing or that of particular assets such as the September 11th terrorist attacks.

exchange
A physical location for trading securities including stocks, bonds, options, and futures.

exchange rate risk
An investment risk term referring to the risk of movement of various currencies in relation to one another and how it can affect the valuation of an investment. Exchange rate risk, or currency risk, comes into play when investors invest in international entities and/or corporations that participate in international business affairs.

expense ratio
Represents the percentage of assets needed to operate a mutual fund or an exchange traded fund, including management, overhead, and distribution costs.

financial market
A system that allows for the buying and selling of financial assets.

financial objectives
Desired end points defined by individuals and entities through financial planning and detailing dollar amounts and time frames.

financial plan
Definition of financial objectives, analysis of existing and future resources, identification of potential disruptions in order to design specific steps to achieve set goals by entities and individuals.

financial planning
The process of developing a financial plan as well as monitoring and adjusting plans over time in order to stay on track for financial objective achievement.

financial risk
The risk that an investment will underperform.

fixed annuity
A contract with an insurance company that requires a deposit by the investor on which the insurer pays interest over time. A fixed annuity is a taxed deferred shell; thus, the investor does not pay taxes on interest until it is withdrawn. Fixed annuities carry an interest rate that is set at the beginning of the contract but can vary over the life of the program.

fixed income investments
An investment that produces a fixed and regular dollar amount such as a bond.

FPPS
Financial Perspectives Planning Services, Inc. was the financial planning firm owned by Bradford C. Bleidt.

fund family
A group of mutual funds offered by one investment entity.

future value
The dollar amount equivalent at a certain future date of a specific sum in today's dollars when factors such as inflation, additions or subtractions, or growth rates are taken into consideration.

global fund
A mutual fund that has the ability to invest throughout the world including the United States.

growth fund
A mutual fund that invests in the common stock of corporations expected to reinvest earnings for expansion purposes.

guaranteed minimum interest rate
A minimal interest rate below which a company cannot reduce the amount it is paying on certain contracts. Frequently used with fixed annuities and universal life insurance contracts.

high yield bond fund
A mutual fund that invests in high yield bonds, often referred to as "junk bonds." High yield bonds carry with them more default risk and thus have higher interest rates to compensate investors than investment grade bonds, which are considered higher quality.

immediate annuity
An income stream provided by an insurance company in return for a specific deposit. The income stream can be defined by the expected lifespan of the investor, a certain time frame, or a combination of the two. Contracts generally become irrevocable after the contract is delivered and the investor has had a defined time to review it.

income statement
An accounting statement of profit detailing income and expenses for an entity or individual.

index fund
A mutual fund that closely matches the investments of an index such as the S&P 500, Russell 2000, and many more including commodity, international, and emerging market indexes. These funds are passively managed and typically carry lower expense ratios than actively managed mutual funds.

inflation
The increase in the general level of prices for goods and services within an economy.

inflation risk
The risk that investment returns will be impacted by inflation levels, sometimes referred to as "purchasing power" risk.

insider information
Nonpublic, material information, positive or negative, about a company that could affect the performance of its stock once made public.

insider trading
The illegal practice of trading a corporation's stock based on nonpublic, material information, which when made public would impact the stock's demand by the investing community.

interest
Compensation paid to an entity that loans money, expressed as a percentage rate.

interest rate risk
The risk that interest rates will affect the value of certain investments, typically bonds. An inverse relationship exists between interest rates

and bond valuations. As interest rates rise, the value of a bond tends to decline and vice versa.

international fund
A mutual fund that invests only internationally and carries no exposure to the United States.

investment grade bond (fund)
A debt instrument that carries an assigned grade within the top four ratings categories from a commercial credit rating company (A.M. Best, Moody's, Standard and Poor's, Fitch). An investment grade bond fund is a fund that invests in these types of securities.

investor
An entity or individual who takes an ownership interest in an asset.

joint account
An account owned by two or more people or entities.

junk bonds
Also known as high yield bonds, junk bonds carry with them more default risk and thus have higher interest rates to compensate investors than investment grade bonds, which are considered higher quality.

large cap stock/mutual fund
A company with a market capitalization between $10 and $200 billion dollars or a mutual fund investing in such companies.

letter of intent
Expresses the promise of an investor to purchase additional shares at some future date in order to qualify for a lower sales charge.

liability
A financial obligation and/or the monetary value of a financial commitment.

liquidity risk
The risk carried by an asset that cannot be bought and sold easily.

load fund
A mutual fund that carries a sales charge upon purchase or over time.

long-term care insurance
Insurance that protects against the high cost of a long-term illness, either in the home or in a facility, beyond what is covered by conventional health insurance.

management fee
Usually determined by the amount of money invested, the management fee compensates an advisor for overseeing investment assets for a client.

margin
Capital that is borrowed from existing investments in order to purchase securities or for other needs.

mark down
An amount earned by a broker/dealer on the purchase of a security from a customer and the price at which the asset can be resold.

mark up
An amount added to the price of a security to compensate the broker and cover transactional costs.

market maker
A financial entity that assists in the stabilization of various securities through buying and selling particular company shares, bringing efficiency and liquidity to the market.

mid cap stock/mutual fund
A company with a market capitalization between $2 and $10 billion dollars or a mutual fund investing in such companies.

mutual fund

A pool of money serving many investors, owning a number of assets that are managed by an investment company. Mutual funds can invest in any number of securities from stocks and bonds to commodities and options.

mutual fund investment style

Indicates the types of securities in which the fund invests and can be represented by a "style box" created by Morningstar. On the equity side, styles include large, medium, and small cap growth; blend; and value. On the fixed income side, styles include high, medium, and low on the quality side with definitions also of short, intermediate, and long maturities.

mutual fund objective

The goal of the mutual fund's investment strategy as stated in its prospectus. Common objectives include aggressive growth, growth, income, balance, international, global, and so on.

net asset value (NAV)

Reflects the market price of a mutual fund without any applicable sales charge.

no-load mutual fund

A mutual fund that does not carry a sales charge. Such funds might or might not have an ongoing distribution charge associated with it.

option

A security that gives the investor the right to buy (call option) or sell (put option) a specified asset at a set price on or before a given date. A buyer of a call asset expects the price of the asset to go up. The buyer of a put option expects the price of the underlying asset to go down.

order
The placement of a security trade request.

passive portfolio management
Utilized by index funds and exchange traded funds where the arrangement of assets within the fund follow that of a certain index such as the S&P 500 or the Russell 2000 or the Europe, Australasia, and Far East indices.

pension plan
Established by an employer entity, a pension plan is a pool of assets developed to provide financial benefits to retirees of the organization.

performance statement
A statement that not only details asset positions and account activity, but also shows performance figures for individual investments as well as the entire portfolio expressed in percentages and usually compared to a relative index.

portfolio
A collection of assets owned by an investor.

portfolio management
The use of a professional to collectively oversee a group of investments. The process typically involves the development of an investment policy statement, analysis of existing assets, asset selection, plan implementation, and ongoing monitoring.

portfolio turnover rate
Expressed as a percentage, this rate gives the investor an idea of how much activity is occurring within a mutual fund or a portfolio. It can be an indicator of whether or not a mutual fund might be prone to a taxable capital gains distribution and also whether or not a broker is involved with churning an account to gain commissions.

proxy
Materials issued by a public company to its shareholders providing the necessary information about stockholders' meeting matters on which investors can vote.

rate of return
The amount of money gained or lost on an amount invested expressed as a percentage.

ratings
Credit evaluation grades provided by A.M. Best, Moody's, Standard & Poor's, and Fitch to help investors and insurance purchasers determine an entity's financial health.

real asset
A physical asset such as real estate, land, and gold.

rebalancing
Adjusting a portfolio through purchases and sales of assets in order to achieve the desired asset allocation. The practice of portfolio rebalancing helps investors systematically sell assets that have appreciated (sell high) and buy others that may be undervalued (buy low).

redemption charge
A charge assessed upon the sale of a mutual fund typically within a certain time frame. The redemption charge is different than the "back end load" or contingent deferred sales charge.

registered representative
An individual who has passed the required examinations and requirements to become licensed to sell securities.

reinvestment risk
The potential that proceeds of the redemption of an investment in the future will be reinvested at a significantly different interest rate.

retirement account

An account that provides tax incentives for individuals to save while they are working in order to build up assets for when they stop working. These accounts provide tax deferral until withdrawn and may furnish investors with tax deductions or tax free withdrawals. 401(k)s, IRAs, Roth IRAs, and tax deferred annuities are all forms of retirement accounts.

risk

The deviation of an expected outcome, either positive or negative, and measured by the standard deviation of a return of an investment.

risk management

The identification and analysis of potential risks and implementation of protective measures in regard to investing as well as one's health, life, and property.

sales charge

Measured by the difference between the purchase price and a mutual fund's net asset value (NAV), the sales charge is a fee encountered when purchasing mutual fund shares that typically pay a broker a commission.

security

An evidential instrument showing investment in a debt or equity asset.

shareholder

An entity or person with ownership shares in a publicly traded company, mutual fund, or exchange traded fund.

shares

Ownership parcels of a publicly traded company, mutual fund, or exchange traded fund.

single premium deferred annuity
An investment with an insurance carrier that requires a deposit by the investor on which the insurance company will pay interest. Deferred annuities carry lengthy "maturity" periods though contracts with shorter surrender or no surrender periods are available. Interest rates can vary over time. The contract holder does not pay taxes on any interest as long as it stays within a deferred annuity shell.

small cap stock/mutual fund
A company with a market capitalization falling approximately between $300 million and $2 billion dollars or a mutual fund investing in such companies.

sovereign risk
The risk that foreign governments will exert their influence and affect the performance of certain investments during volatile economic and political periods.

stock
Equity ownership in a corporation via shared ownership.

stock dividend
A corporate dividend issued in the form of additional shares in a corporation or one that is being spun off from the company.

stock exchange
An organization made up of member firms formed for the purpose of trading shares of stock.

stockholder
An entity or person with ownership shares in a publicly traded company.

systematic risk
Risk that is attributable to overall risks associated with existing markets.

tax deferred annuity
A retirement vehicle with an insurance carrier that requires a deposit by the investor on which the insurance company will pay interest. Deferred annuities carry lengthy "maturity" periods though contracts with shorter surrender or no surrender periods are available. Interest rates can vary over time. The contract holder does not pay taxes on any interest as long as it stays within a deferred annuity shell.

term life insurance
A pure death benefit insurance vehicle that does not provide any cash value over the life of the contract. The term of the contract is expressed in years.

turnover
Applicable to portfolios of assets including mutual funds, turnover is a percentage equal to the value of asset trades divided by the average total of portfolio assets. Turnover can be an indicator of churning in a portfolio or potential capital gain exposure in a mutual fund.

universal life insurance
A flexible insurance product that can accumulate cash values over time. The owner can, within limits, change premium investments and death benefits over time. As long as the premiums and interest being credited to the policy are more than the mortality and other charges associated with the contract, the insurance coverage should not lapse.

value stock/mutual fund
A company whose trading price is seemingly undervalued or a mutual fund that invests in such companies.

variable annuity (VA)

An annuity contract that allows the investor to choose various "sub-accounts," which are usually reflective of existing security indexes and mutual funds. VAs also may offer death and living benefit contract riders for additional cost to the investor.

variable life insurance

A whole or universal life insurance policy that utilizes "sub-accounts," which are usually reflective of existing security indexes and mutual funds instead of interest and dividends in order to derive cash value performance.

whole life insurance

Permanent life insurance that accumulates cash values via interest payments and dividends and supports a death benefit when designed properly and adequate premium payments are added.

Index

Numerics

1099R, 7

1099s, 7

12B-1 fees, 45, 167

A

A shares, 37

AAII (American Association of Individual Investors), 156

AAMS (Accredited Asset Management Specialist), 22

AARP (American Association of Retired Persons), 156

accessibility to financial advisors, 135

Accredited Asset Management Specialist (AAMS), 22

Accredited Financial Counselor (AFC), 22

activity, 131-132

administrative and management fees

annuities, 45

ETFs, 46

index funds, 46

mutual funds, 45

advisor-client relationships, 127-130

advisors (financial advisors), 18, 77

accessibility, 135

to avoid, 107-109

checking out, 101-103

choosing, 77-79

interviewing, 81-82

compensation, 31, 47-48

combination fee and commission, 33

fee offset, 33

fee only, 32

financial planning, 50

insurance coverage, 49

investment-related, 48-49

transactions, 31

dysfunctional relationships with, 137-140

example of what they do, 118-120

interviewing

after meeting, 97-99

during meeting, 92-96

preparing for meeting, 85-86, 89-92

red flags after meeting, 106-107

red flags during meeting, 104-106

AFC (Accredited Financial
Counselor), 22
AFSAEF (American Financial
Services Association
Education Foundation), 156
AICPA (American Institute
for Certified Public
Accountants), 157
AIE (Alliance for Investor
Education), 155
A.M. Best, 163
American Association of
Individual Investors
(AAII), 156
American Association of
Retired Persons (AARP), 156
American Financial Services
Association Education
Foundation (AFSAEF), 156
American Institute for
Certified Public Accountants
(AICPA), 157
annual maintenance fees, 43-44
annuities, 44
annual reports, 55
annualcreditreport.com, 164
annuities
fees, 44-45
fixed annuities, 41
compensation for
financial advisors, 49
immediate annuities, 59-61
indexed annuities, fees, 41

living benefits, 40
variable annuities
compensation for
financial advisors, 48
fees, 39
prospectuses, 56
arbitration, 153-154
asset agreements, 111-113
asset management
compensation for financial
advisors, 48
fees, 35
asset managers, 120
information they may need,
123-124
asset sale information, 52
assets
investment risk tolerance,
121-122
transferring, 124

B

B shares, 38
balance sheets, 75-76, 90
Bernard L. Madoff
Investment Securities,
LLC, 11
Bleidt, Bradford C., 1-8
Board of Governors of the
Federal Reserve, 157
bonds, fees, 36

breach of contract, 138
breakpoints, 39
broker/dealers, 6-7, 63-64
brokerages, fees, 43-44

C

C shares, 38
cash flow, 15
  budgeting and, 68, 72
CDSC (contingent deferred sales charges), 38
Certified Financial Board of Standards, Inc., 157
CERTIFIED FINANCIAL PLANNER™ professional, 18
Certified Financial Planner Board of Standards, Inc., 79
Certified Fund Specialist (CFS), 24
Certified Investment Management Analyst (CIMA), 24
Certified Public Accountants (CPAs), 19
Certified Trust and Financial Advisor (CTFA), 26
CFA (Chartered Financial Analyst), 21
CFA Institute, 157
CFP® professional, 21

CFS (Certified Fund Specialist), 24
chain letters, 146
charges, standard charges on contracts, 56
Chartered Financial Analyst (CFA), 21
Chartered Financial Consultant (ChFC), 21
Chartered Investment Counselor (CIC), 24
Chartered Life Underwriter (CLU), 25
Chartered Retirement Plans Specialist (CRPS), 25
check/credit card fees, 44
checking out financial advisors, 101-103
checks, rules for, 5
ChFC (Chartered Financial Consultant), 21
choosing financial advisors, 77-79
  interviewing candidates, 81-82
churning, 138. *See also* activity, 131-132
CIC (Chartered Investment Counselor), 24
CIMA (Certified Investment Management Analyst), 24
closure fees, 43

CLU (Chartered Life Underwriter), 25

college funding, 69, 72

commission, 31

mutual funds, 37-39

commission schedules, 36

communication, 90

dysfunctional relationships with advisors, 137

compensation, financial advisors, 47-48

financial planning, 50

insurance coverage, 49

investment-related, 48-49

compensation for advisors, 31

combination fee and commission, 33

fee offset, 33

fee only, 32

transactions, 31

complaints

arbitration, 153-154

filing, 149-154

confirmations, 5, 37

Consumer Federation of America, 158

contingent deferred sales charges (CDSC), 38

contracts, standard charges, 56

cost basis information, 52

Coverdell Education Savings Account (ESA), 69

CPAs (Certified Public Accountants), 19, 22

checking out, 103

credit ratings agencies, 163-164

credit reports, 164-165

criminal activity, chain letters, 146

criminal behavior, 144-147, 150-151

multi-level marketing schemes, 146

offshore, 147

Ponzi schemes, 145

pump and dump, 147

pyramid schemes, 146

CRPS (Chartered Retirement Plans Specialist), 25

CTFA (Certified Trust and Financial Advisor), 26

custodians, 64

D

Defined Benefit retirement programs, 16

Defined Contribution programs, 16

discretionary authority, 129

dysfunctional relationships with advisors, 137-140

E

e-statements, 51
education funding, 16
egoists, 140
Equifax, 165
ESA (Coverdell Education Savings Account), 69
estate planning, 17, 67, 71
ETFs (Exchange Traded Funds)
   administrative and management fees, 46
   fees, 36
example of what financial advisors do, 118-120
Experian, 165

F

family structure, 86
FDIC (Federal Deposit Insurance Company), 65, 158
Federal Trade Commission's Bureau of Consumer Protection, 158
fee and commission, compensation for advisors, 33
fee offset, compensation for advisors, 33
fee only, compensation for advisors, 32
fees, 34
   12B-1, 45
   administrative and management fees, 45
   annual maintenance, annuities, 44
   annuities, 44-45
   asset management, 35
   bonds, 36
   check/credit card, 44
   closure, 43
   ETFs, 36, 46
   financial planning, 36
   inactivity, 44
   index funds, 46
   indexed annuities, 41
   insurance, 41-42
   investment change, 57
   mailing fees, 44
   managed and/or brokerage, 43-44
   margin interest, 44
   mortality and expenses, 44
   mutual funds, 37-39, 45
   portfolio development, 35
   redemption, 45
   retirement accounts, 43
   riders, 44

stocks, 36
surrender, 45
ticket charges, 44
variable annuities, 39
wiring, 44
filing complaints, 149-154
financial advisors, 18
  accessibility, 135
  to avoid, 107-109
  checking out, 101-103
  choosing, 77-79
    interviewing, 81-82
  compensation, 31, 47-48
    combination fee and com-
      mission, 33
    fee offset, 33
    fee only, 32
    financial planning, 50
    insurance coverage, 49
    investment-related, 48-49
    transactions, 31
  dysfunctional relationships
    with, 137-140
  example of what they do,
    118-120
  interviewing
    after meeting, 97-99
    during meeting, 92-96
    preparing for meeting,
      85-86, 89-92

  red flags after meeting,
    106-107
  red flags during meeting,
    104-106
financial goals, 87
Financial Industry Regulatory
  Authority (FINRA), 28, 64,
  81, 158
financial institutions, 59
financial planners, 18
financial planning, 15-17,
  69-71
  cash flow, 15
  compensation for financial
    advisors, 50
  education funding, 16
  estate planning, 17
  fees, 36
  information advisor will
    need, 117
  retirement, 16
  risk management, 16
  taxation, 15
Financial Planning
  Agreements, 113-114, 116
Financial Planning Association
  (FPA), 79, 159
financial plans, reviewing, 116
FINRA (Financial Industry
  Regulatory Authority), 28,
  64, 81, 158
  filing complaints, 153

FINRA Complaints and
Tips, 149
Fitch Ratings, Ltd., 163
fixed annuities, 41
compensation for financial
advisors, 49
Form ADV, 98, 102, 112
Foundation for Investor
Education, 159
FPA (Financial Planning
Association), 159
fraud, 138

G-H-I

goals, 87

home offices, 7

IARs (Investment Advisor
Representatives), 20, 65, 102
ICAA (Investment Counsel
Association of America), 24
ICI (Investment Company
Institute), 159
illegal activity, 150-151
IMCA (Investment
Management Consultants
Association), 159
immediate annuities, 59, 61
inactivity, 132-133
inactivity fees, 44
income statements, 73-74,
87-88

incompetent advisors, 140
index funds, fees, 46
indexed annuities, fees, 41
information asset managers
may need, 123-124
information financial advisors
may need, 117
insurance
fees, 41-42
investments in, 61-63
mutual insurance
companies, 61
risk management, 68, 72
stock insurance companies, 61
universal life, 61, 184
variable life, 62, 185
whole life, 61, 185
insurance coverage
compensation, financial
advisors, 49
insurance purchases, 127
insurance representatives, 19
interviewing financial
advisors, 81-82
after meeting, 97-99
during meeting, 92-96
preparing for meeting,
85-86, 89-92
red flags after meeting,
106-107
red flags during meeting,
104-106

Investment Advisor
Representatives (IARs),
20, 65, 102

investment asset details, 91

investment change fees, 57

Investment Company
Institute (ICI), 159

Investment Counsel
Association of America
(ICAA), 24

Investment Management
Agreements, 111-113

Investment Management
Consultants Association
(IMCA), 159

investment purchases, 128

investment representatives, 19

investment risk tolerance,
121-122

investment scammers,
147-148

investment strategies, 68, 71

investment-related
compensation, financial
advisors, 48-49

investments in insurance
products, 61-63

Investor Protector Trust, 160

K-L

Keefe, James, 99

Lee, Dee, 16

licenses
Series 6, 28
Series 7, 28
Series 24, 28
Series 26, 28
Series 63, 28
Series 65, 29
Series 66, 29
state insurance, 28

living benefits, annuities, 40

loaded products, 47

M

Madoff, Andrew, 9

Madoff, Bernard, 8-12,
92, 145

Madoff, Mark, 9

mailing fees, 44

maintaining advisor-client
relationships, 127-130

managed fees, 43-44

margin interest, fees, 44

misrepresentation, 138

Moody's Investor
Services, 164

mortality and expenses,
fees, 44

multi-level marketing, 146

mutual funds
   A shares, 37
   B shares, 38
   C shares, 38
   fees, 37-39, 45
mutual insurance
   companies, 61

N

NAIC (National Association of
   Insurance Commissioners),
   160
NASAA (North American
   Securities Administrators
   Association), 149, 161
National Association of
   Insurance Commissioners
   (NAIC), 160
National Association of
   Investors Corporation, 160
National Association of
   Personal Financial
   Advisors, 79
National Endowment for
   Financial Education
   (NEFE), 161
National Foundation
   for Credit Counseling
   (NFCC), 161
NEFE (National Endowment
   for Financial Education), 161
negligence, 138

net worth, 75-76
New York Stock Exchange
   (NYSE), 161
NFCC (National Foundation
   for Credit Counseling), 161
North American Securities
   Administrators Association
   (NASAA), 149, 161
NYSE (New York Stock
   Exchange), 161

O-P

offshore, 147
OSJ (Office of Supervisory
   Jurisdiction), 132, 138
paperwork, 124
PFS (Personal Financial
   Specialist), 26
Ponzi schemes, 145
portfolio development
   compensation for financial
   advisors, 48
   fees, 35
portfolio development fee, 33
prospectuses, 53-55
   variable annuities, 56
proxy cards, 58
proxy materials, 57
proxy voting, 112
pump and dump, 147
pyramid schemes, 146

Q-R

questions to ask while interviewing financial advisors, 94

red flags, 102, 144
after meeting, 106-107
during meeting, 104-106
dysfunctional relationships, 137
financial advisors to avoid, 107-109
financial professionals to avoid, 143

redemption fees, 45

referrals, 106

Registered Financial Consultant (RFC), 27

Registered Investment Advisors (RIAs), 20, 65, 102

relationships
advisor-client relationships, 127-130
dysfunctional relationships with advisors, 137-140

researching RIAs, 102

retainers, compensation for financial advisors, 50

retirement, 68, 72
financial planning, 16

retirement accounts, fees, 43

reviewing
financial plans, 116
statements, 52

RFC (Registered Financial Consultant), 27

RIAs (Registered Investment Advisors), 20, 65, 102
researching, 102

rider electives, 57

riders, fees, 44

risk, investment risk tolerance, 121-122

risk management, 16
insurance, 68, 72

S

scam artists, 1

SEC (Securities and Exchange Commission), 37, 63, 81, 163

SEC Complaint Center, 149

Securities Industry and Financial Markets Association, 162

Securities Investment Protection Corporation (SIPC), 66, 162

Series 6, 28

Series 7, 28

Series 24, 28

Series 26, 28

Series 63, 28
Series 65, 29
Series 66, 29
service charges on trades, 44
shareholder updates, 55
SIPC (Securities Investment Protection Corporation), 66, 162
skepticism, 144
Social Security Administration (SSA), 162
Squillari, Eleanor, 8, 12
SSA (Social Security Administration), 162
Standard and Poor's, 164
state insurance license, 28
statements, 51-53
    income, 73-74
    reviewing, 52
stock insurance companies, 61
stocks, fees, 36
sub-account expenses, 57
surrender charges, 57
surrender fees, 45

T

tax laws, 15
tax planning, 67, 71
taxation, 15
thieves, financial advisors, 140

ticket charges, fees, 44
traded securities, compensation for financial advisors, 48
transactions, compensation for advisors, 31
transferring assets, 124
Transunion, 165

U-Z

U.S. Department of the Treasury, 162
U.S. Securities and Exchange Commission (SEC), 163
universal life insurance, 41, 61
unsuitability, 139

variable annuities
    compensation for financial advisors, 48
    fees, 39
    prospectuses, 56
variable life insurance, 62
voting items, 58

whole life insurance, 41
wiring fees, 44

FINANCIAL TIMES

In an increasingly competitive world, it is quality of thinking that gives an edge—an idea that opens new doors, a technique that solves a problem, or an insight that simply helps make sense of it all.

We work with leading authors in the various arenas of business and finance to bring cutting-edge thinking and best-learning practices to a global market.

It is our goal to create world-class print publications and electronic products that give readers knowledge and understanding that can then be applied, whether studying or at work.

To find out more about our business products, you can visit us at www.ftpress.com.